REPORTING/ WRITING/EDITING

The Quill Guides to Journalism

Series editor: **Ron Lovell**

Editors of this volume: **Ron Dorfman**
Harry Fuller, Jr.

The Society of Professional Journalists,
Sigma Delta Chi

**KENDALL/HUNT
PUBLISHING COMPANY**
Dubuque, Iowa

B   402832   01

Contents

Preface

Authority and believability. The journalist needs these qualities to perform the service of news gathering and news presentation for the public.

These qualities are not attainable unless the journalist is professional, working under accepted standards, ethics, techniques, principles and responsibilities, has reverence for facts, respect for language, acquires skills and develops an uncompromising integrity.

The purposes of the Society of Professional Journalists, Sigma Delta Chi are no more complex than the ingredients of that statement. They were the concerns of the ten college students who founded the Greek letter fraternity at DePauw University in Greencastle, Indiana in 1909. A portion of their initiation ceremony serves today to reflect the highest standards in journalism: ". . . a profession based on freedom to learn and publish the facts; . . . that is as jealous of the right to utter unpopular opinions as of the privilege to agree with the majority; . . . that lays its own claim to service on a vigilance that knows no midnight and a courage that knows no retreat."

During 1982, the Society enrolled its 100,000th member since 1909. It admits to membership the greatest names in journalism, but is, at the same time, the most representative national press organization, including student and teacher of journalism, beginning reporter and publisher, anchorman and overnight rewrite person, in newspapers, magazines, wire services, television and radio.

Its causes are substantive. The Society vigorously supports the highest standards of journalism education and mid-career continuing education, recognizes achievement and excellence of outstanding journalists, promotes ethics and advances the cause of freedom of information. The Code of Ethics of the Society, adopted in 1926 and revised in 1973, is a clear statement of the independence of the press and the need for objectivity, accuracy and fairness. The free press issue requires substantial time, energy and financial resources by a large portion of the leadership and membership.

The national organization consists of nearly 140 professional and more than 175 campus chapters, and has more than 28,000 members. National headquarters is located in Chicago, Illinois.

A vital priority of the Society is the monthly magazine, *The Quill,* a respected voice of the professional since 1912. *The Quill* observes and criticizes journalism. Many of its articles deal with the art and craft of reporting, writing and editing. This volume, first in a series, centers on these subjects, hopefully furthering the Society's interests in professionalism through the words on its pages.

> Russell C. Tornabene,
> Executive Officer,
> Society of Professional Journalists,
> Sigma Delta Chi

Acknowledgments

The editor wishes to acknowledge former *Quill* editors Charles Long and Naomi Donson for their work in editing the articles in this book before they were originally published in the magazine.

Introduction

This book represents a milestone for the Society of Professional Journalists, Sigma Delta Chi. More importantly, it represents the beginning of a process of magnifying the potentially valuable journalistic messages presented over the years by *The Quill*, the Society's magazine for journalists.

It is a marriage of two important components of the Society's mission—*The Quill* magazine with its historic contributions to the professional development of journalists and a newer commitment to the same goal through support of continuing education opportunities. Through his work on this book, Ron Lovell has sought to overcome the *Quill*'s natural limitations of time and space. He has succeeded, selecting articles by knowledgeable professionals and journalism educators. This book is a source of nonperishable guidance, helpful to students or working newspersons in the endless search for improved journalistic skills.

It is no accident that this first book in *The Quill* series is on the subjects of reporting, writing and editing. It is not true that journalism has recently discovered the value of good writing, but it is true that recent times have brought renewed and increased emphasis on the subject.

Writing coaches, editors' conferences and critiques and outside consultants are making their presence felt more strongly in newsrooms—print and broadcast—across the nation. Reporters and editors informally and formally discuss writing techniques. The eye for good writing always has been there, but its 20–20 quality has become more sharply focused.

James P. Gannon, executive editor of the Des Moines, Iowa *Register and Tribune,* is among those who have spoken of the trend. "What does a newspaper have to offer the reader if not good stories well-told?" he recently asked in *The Bulletin of the American Society of Newspaper Editors.* "Perhaps we are getting back to the basics of good reporting and writing after realizing the folly of competing on the other guy's terms. What readers want from newspapers is news. And they want it written in a way that won't confuse them, bore them or waste their precious time. They want writing that clarifies complex issues, writing that illuminates people, places and things with the subtle light of well-used language, writing that builds on a rock-solid foundation of fact and a structure of clear thinking with the tools and the trimming of well-chosen words."

It is not true that the manner of presentation is as significant to the reader, listener or viewer as the quality of the information. But it is undeniable that the value received depends to a great degree upon how the presentation commands attention.

The goal, of course, is to combine good writing with quality information. That's no secret. But doing this requires intense concentration by reporters and editors in the face of information overloads and time shortages.

But this need for good writing—as well as the need for reporters and editors to understand better the subject matter with which they deal—also requires that opportunities be provided for continued learning and skill development. The same can be said for the subject of reporting and editing.

We are long past the day in which it is necessary to prove the importance of continuing education programs for journalists. One will find near-universal acceptance of the belief that a more complex society requires that journalists have broader understanding of that society and of the human and social institutions functioning within it.

Criticism of the journalistic product often contains the charge that reporters and editors do not understand complexities of materials with which they deal, be that business, education, politics, or nuclear physics. Even keeping in mind the obvious fact that many of these critics' statements are self-serving, enough truth lies within the charge to cause concern. Journalists themselves often will admit their limitations.

This challenge is being faced, although slowly and, at times, cautiously. Journalistic organizations sponsor special programs, sometimes nationally, but often regionally or locally. Colleges and universities offer opportunities for reporters to return to campuses for several months to retool generally or for short-term seminars on specialized subjects. Among the most popular of these subjects have been law, economics, energy and the environment, public documents, politics and writing development.

Employers are more likely to allow time and funds so that reporters may take advantage of such opportunities. That's the context into which SPJ,SDX in the past few years has structured its effort. This organization, like others, has long been involved in professional development. It has sought to contribute to advancing higher standards of performance, ethics and understanding. As Virginia Commonwealth University faculty member Charles Fair says, "The Society of Professional Journalists, Sigma Delta Chi didn't just turn over a rock this year and discover the need for continuing education for journalists. National and regional conferences of the Society have dealt with a variety of career-enrichment topics, and for some years now, professional and campus chapters have been conducting worshops and seminars on journalistic skills and problems."

But perhaps former national president Howard Graves, chief of bureau for the Associated Press in Portland, Oregon, put the need for evaluation of the Society's commitment into the strongest perspective: "In today's world of ethical problems and too-frequent examples of faulty journalism," he says, "this Society can be a leader in providing opportunities for all journalists to improve the execution of their craft. It's an effort in which we should step out, be bold and creative. There's ample room for SPJ in continuing education, and there's certainly a crying need. It's a move which would be welcomed by graduating students, young reporters, seasoned veterans—those who belong to SPJ and those who do not. We serve all of America's journalists, and what we do reflects on everyone."

To this end, the Society—through its Education Committee and other arms, including individual chapters—has sought to join with those who would make developmental opportunities available to journalists. The main early thrust of that effort has been sponsorship of various programs, often in concert with other organizations. The effort, to this point, has been small, but it represents a beginning of what national officers, the board of directors and headquarters staff hope will signify growing future developments.

Among plans in the original proposal for this effort is development of resources for journalists, more specifically that "funds be allocated and efforts be devoted to building a library of resources" with "attention being devoted to commissioning SPJ-produced materials."

This book, then, is the beginning of a new phase of the SPJ,SDX effort. Other books and materials will follow in its path. We appreciate the opportunity to make it available. We hope its readers find it useful.

Ralph S. Izard, Ohio University
Chairman, Education Committee,
Society of Professional
Journalists, Sigma Delta Chi

Reporting

*Confidential sources are vital to effective investigative re-
porting. . . . (There are) perils involved in using confidential
sources. The perils can become very personal and very costly.*

Clark Mollenhoff

In over 35 years as a Washington investigative reporter, Clark Mollenhoff learned how to deal with confidential sources, sometimes the hard way—by making mistakes. In this March 1979 article, Mollenhoff, now teaching journalism at Washington and Lee University, offers five rules for working with such sources. Since Watergate's "Deep Throat," the use of unnamed sources has increased greatly. At first this practice added to the glamour and sometimes danger of journalism. Now it may bring ethical and legal problems down on the heads of reporters. Mollenhoff's first rule seems slightly more crucial than the others, and the one reporters violate most often.

A PRIMER FOR REPORTERS: YOU'D BETTER KNOW WHAT YOU'RE GETTING INTO

Clark R. Mollenhoff

Confidential sources are vital to effective investigative reporting. That you know already. What you'd better know also are the perils involved in using confidential sources. The perils can become very personal and very costly.

1

DON'T BE TOO quick to offer or give blanket assurances of confidentiality. Consider the source. Give serious attention to the value of the information. Think of the possible consequences: *Is publication (or even retention without publication) worth the risk to me and my employer in the event criminal indictments are returned against the subject of my story? How is my employer likely to respond if he and I are brought to court? Fighting for a principle could be too expensive for him. I could go to jail.*

2

IF YOU'RE TRULY sincere about protecting the identity of your source, don't accentuate the fact that you have one. If you must say anything in your story in which you rely on a single secret source, say "The Tribune has learned that. . . ." To tell your readers or listeners you have a confidential source is to wave a red flag in the faces of defense attorneys, prosecutors, police officials and judges. A thorough search through public records will often prove you don't have to use your confidential source at all in your story. Information from public records can serve to corroborate your root source. Further protection can be had from quotable sources that are not confidential. In other words, do everything within your power to obscure the fact that you have a confidential source. And that means don't keep notes that might identify him or her.

3

THE DECISIONS of this U.S. Supreme Court hold that there is no First Amendment right of a newsman to withhold testimony or documents from a grand jury, the courts or law enforcement officials. Wigmore on Evidence (legal authority John Henry Wigmore) says the state, in the interest of ascertaining truth, is entitled to every person's evidence. If every person includes the president of the United States (which it does), it also includes a reporter or an editor or a radio-TV news director. In the Nixon tapes case, the Supreme Court said the president has only "a presumption" of executive privilege in protecting his confidentiality. That presumption, the Court said, must give way when the available evidence indicates crimes have been committed. In ruling 5–4 in *Branzburg v. Hayes* in 1972, the Supreme Court refused to establish either an absolute or a qualified newsman's privilege based on the First Amendment. But those opinions the Court did leave to the discretion of the U.S. Congress and the state legislatures.

4

IT IS WRONG to tell your source your communications are protected by a shield law or the First Amendment. Under the present state of law, that would be a misrepresentation. Shield laws adopted for the protection of the newsman's privilege do exist in 26 states in various forms. But in the face of inquiries from police, prosecutors, grand jurors and others, their benefits to newsmen are, at best, limited. The Farber case demonstrates, even dramatizes, that a shield law is not, nor is it likely to be, any real protection for a reporter when the law comes in conflict with what a judge determines to be the Sixth Amendment right of a defendant "to have compulsory process for obtaining witnesses in his favor. . . ." All you can assure your source is that you will go to jail rather than betray your confidentiality.

5

WHETHER YOU like it or not, you will have to live with the reality of the bench's concern for the Sixth Amendment and stop dreaming of any special status as a journalist. A nation unwilling to give an unqualified executive privilege to the president is not very likely to approve an absolute privilege to someone who calls himself a journalist. But even if a legal privilege were forthcoming, there's something else to think on. Given to lawmakers to decide, how would a "journalist" be defined? Would the definition, for example, include the neighborhood pamphleteer as well as the editor of a metropolitan newspaper?

A FOOTNOTE: Don't sign a contract to write a book that is related in any manner to your confidential source until all litigation is concluded. Even if you are pure of heart in your motivation, the existence of any contractual arrangement provides attorneys, judges or any other critics with an argument that you have a financial stake in the outcome of a trial. It can leave the impression you are remaining silent for a price rather than a principle.

A recent sin of the press has been the widespread use of confidential sources, often when it isn't really necessary. In this March 1979 article, Jerry Chaney, a journalism professor at Ball State University, questions "the ironbound tenet that the press has an absolute right to keep sources confidential." He thinks this invites public suspicion of the press unnecessarily. In keeping the names of sources secret, reporters demand that readers accept without question everything they report. This is a posture journalists would not think of taking with any other institution.

LEVEL WITH US, JUST HOW SACRED IS YOUR SOURCE?

Jerry Chaney

My heretical suggestion will send quivers of nervous revulsion through many of my colleagues in the press. So be it.

We journalists should disown our ironbound tenet that the press has an absolute right to keep sources confidential. When you think about it, this never was a sound idea.

Consider the tenet's chief defense: to protect the anonymity of sources who do not wish to be identified. These sources, therefore, feel free to speak. And the interest of disseminating information the public has a right to know is thereby served.

What does that mean? It certainly doesn't mean that the public's right to know always includes the right to know sources. And that can only mean that journalists want the public to believe that journalists have too much integrity to use sources in a way that is deceptive.

In other words, journalists are saying to the public, "Trust us"—a posture, incidentially, that journalists will not tell the public to assume of any other institution.

But why shouldn't the public wonder about possible deception in the press accounts they see and hear? It takes no mental giant to figure out that being told who supplied the information could be as important as what the informant had to say. Knowing the source affects credibility, both as to the source's qualifications for giving the information and as to possible bias.

Indeed, the addition of a source's identity to a story could cast the story in an entirely different light, perhaps causing the reader or viewer to make an assessment exactly opposite of what he or she otherwise would have made. As a former student of mine once observed, "I guess knowing whether the president of the company or the janitor said it could make a lot of difference."

It takes little effort to find examples of what we're talking about:

• A story in the Christian Science Monitor, concerning the meeting of President Sadat and Prime Minister Begin at Camp David, cited an "expert" five times as the source of information. In fact, nowhere in the story was a source identified by name. Other sources were identified as "administration officials," "key Arab parties" and "senior Arab diplomats."

• A copyrighted story by Anthony Marro of the Washington Star on the pending trial of William P. Kampiles, who was accused and subsequently convicted of turning over a top-secret manual to a Soviet agent, contained at least six references to unnamed sources. They were: "one intelligence officer," "one former CIA officer," "one defense systems expert," "a number of sources," "several Justice Department sources" and "one government source." The article also used the expression "is said" without telling who did the saying.

• An Associated Press story on Iraq contained information attributed to the following: "some knowledgeable Iraqis," "longtime foreign-residents," "most observers" and "analysts."

• A United Press International story on the politics and policy of China contained such attributions as "knowledgeable U.S. officials," "independent China scholars" and "China experts."

• A New York Times News Service story on alleged Soviet involvement in the overthrow of the Shah of Iran attributed information to such veiled sources as "a senior intelligence officer," "a Western envoy," "a moderate opposition figure," "a British expatriat," "a European intelligence source" and the ever-popular "informed source."

• A copyrighted Los Angeles Times story by George McArthur on corruption in Vietnam attributed information to such as "some responsible authorities outside Vietnam," "refugee officials," "refugees," and another favorite standby, "a senior American official."

One could get the impression the public is often left in the dark as to who supplied the press with its information. Research reported in the fall of 1978 issue of Journalism Quarterly indicated that indefinite or veiled attribution was "common" in newspapers and occurred in 70 percent of Newsweek stories and 75 percent of Time magazine stories.

For the press successfully to defend its self-invited role as servant of the public's right to know, it had better realize that the right is rapidly becoming a two-way street. As the press continues to dish out information to the public as it chooses, the public, in turn, is demonstrating a stronger inclination to demand substantiation.

Meeting that demand shouldn't be all that hard to accomplish if only the press would put more pressure on those hiding behind their names to go public.

Most confidential sources, from this writer's experience, want their information to be published because it serves their special interests. And they want their names kept secret simply because they know public knowledge of their identities would weaken what they have to say. Most of this type of source should be forced with either going public or going unpublished. From this writer's experience, most of them would opt for the former and not suffer consequent injury either to themselves or to innocent persons involved.

When it is necessary to exclude the identity of a source (or anyone else in a story) because of probable injury, this should be explained in the story as fully as possible without betraying the source. And that is a suggestion to end this discussion on not so heretical a note, for the Associated Press Managing Editors says as much in its own code of ethics.

When the results of public opinion polls first appeared in the media, they were largely to report preferences for presidential candidates. Indeed, polls are the pivotal point of the "horse race" aspect of national campaigns the public seems to enjoy. More recently, however, public opinion polls on many subjects have become a regular staple of everyday coverage. The plethora of polls has brought with it an inaccuracy and lack of quality editors would never tolerate from reporters, says Penn State journalism professor John N. Rippey in this October 1979 article. After outlining some examples of poor poll stories, Rippey notes ways to improve them.

THE HARD NEWS ABOUT CAREFULLY CRAFTED POLL STORIES— AND THOSE THAT AREN'T

John N. Rippey

Public opinion polling by newspapers, radio and television has increased greatly during the past decade, and the sophistication of journalists about this social science research tool has also increased. However, for a business that prides itself on the accuracy of its news product, the news business often regards polls as simply good copy.

It appears that sloppily conducted news polls are the result of a willingness by some news executives to us poll stories that they feel are *accurate* enough. This is a philosophy that can be rationalized for hard-news reporting, when deadlines force publication or broadcast and if the reader, viewer or listener is properly alerted that not all of the facts were available. But there is no excuse for using stories about polls that are unlikely to be representative or do not take elementary safeguards to maximize accuracy.

Reputable news outlets that go to considerable lengths to report accurately and fairly what is going on at City Hall should take the same care with public opinion—both in doing their own polls and in reporting polls from other sources. Statistical methods are available that should make measurement of public attitudes more accurate than many public affairs stories from frequently subjective sources at City Hall.

If newspapers and broadcasters really mean what they say about accuracy, they should do their polls under professionally accepted guidelines. As Sidney H. Hurlburt, executive editor of the Burlington (Vt.) Free Press, puts it: "It is my judgment that in polling it is preferable to go first class or not to go at all. Newspapers and broadcast media which commission or conduct small-sample polls (with the resulting sharp increase in error range), or fail to solicit professional advice in framing the question, or—worst of all—set up some self-selecting response mechanism with its resulting unscientific result and call it a poll, give all the rest of us a bad name."

Consider two headlines:

PEACE TREATY SECONDARY
TO OIL PRICE IN SURVEY

and

SUNDAY STORE HOURS FAVORED
BY 62% OF 2,735 SURVEYED

The first headline does not tell the reader this was a survey of the street-corner variety, a notoriously unrepresentative measure of public opinion. The story that follows the headline does not even say how many persons were interviewed. Five are quoted and four of them are pictured.

The second headline does not tell the reader that the 2,735 persons "surveyed" selected themselves to be in the sample by clipping a questionnaire from the paper and mailing it in.

The first story did not, to its credit, claim that it represented the attitudes of the community, and the second story was, in fact, preceded by an editor's note that the "reader opinion survey on Sunday retail store hours was not intended to be a statistically accurate model . . . its sole purpose was to provide people the opportunity to air their opinions in an unofficial public forum." Nevertheless, it is difficult for most readers to distinguish between a story that describes the attitudes of a representative sample and one that simply titillates with the colorful quotes of passerbys—or worse, perhaps, one whose percentages and raw figures give the impression the story is based on a "scientific" poll.

In a survey of daily newspapers in the United States, I found that about one-third of them said they had conducted opinion polls to gather information on which to base stories. (The mail survey was done in 1978 using a randomly selected sample of 817 dailies; responses came from 53 percent.) Most of the smaller dailies, with limited resources, depend entirely on their own staffs to design and conduct polls. This finding, along with other evidence from the survey, led me to suspect that a certain percentage of the papers, especially the smaller ones, were doing a poor job of polling.

The editors responsible for the two stories cited above were among those who responded to a follow-up among papers of less than 50,000 circulation in which I attempted to obtain some examples—rather than statistics—of what was going on out there. I did not need a computer printout to convince me that misleading poll results passed on to readers even once is journalistically significant.

The two editors who supplied the poll headlines offered contrasting comments on how they conducted their polls. One apparently does not know what a valid poll is; the other apparently does.

The editor who ran the street-corner poll on the price of oil explained: "Our method of conducting a poll is quite scientific. We go out and ask the people what they think of a given subject. We've found the best place for doing this is where we find them—at the coffee shops, in the shopping centers and at the post office. We take a couple of mug shots and go with what we've got, using the credence that spot checks show a sample of what people are thinking." This is the classic rationale for the man-in-the-street poll. Few journalists today would defend it as "scientific."

By contrast, the editor's note preceding the poll story on Sunday store hours reveals that this young editor has some idea of what a "statistically accurate model" is and isn't. Why did this newspaper not do it right, then? The editor approached the project with commendable zeal. He originated the idea, wrote all of the promotional materials, did all the tabulations, wrote all of the related stories.

"This job of compiling all the responses was a true demonic possession for nearly 12 hours in one sitting," he said. For this obviously sincere effort, it would seem that the readers deserved a poll they could trust.

Other editors wrote comments about their polls that indicated they, too, should have known better.

The editor of a daily with less than 5,000 circulation wrote that his methodology was "admittedly unscientific." His five staff members divided up the phone books and tried to make what they thought was a random selection of numbers. They made all of their calls in the afternoon; most of the responses were from housewives.

Another editor wrote that his paper's methods of polling "could hardly be described as being scientific." His staff, too, drew numbers randomly from the phone book. The number of contacts ranged from 10 to 100, depending on the poll, and was, as the editor repeated, "hardly a scientific formula." Yet, such polls were conducted with the paper's belief they would "make the foundation for a news story." Would this same editor tell his staff to go out and knowingly collect flawed facts as the foundation for any other kind of story?

Guidelines on reporting polls have been advanced by such a variety of sources as the American Association for Public Opinion Research, the National Council on Public Polls, the Associated Press Managing Editors, the Canadian Daily Newspaper Publishers Association, and the Gannetteer, the magazine for Gannett Co. employees.

Increased public polling is high on the list of priorities at Sidney Hurlburt's Burlington Free Press. It is a priority that wasn't made without some consideration to cost. Hurlburt said that commissioning a poll from a private firm to conduct 800 interviews is, as he put it, not cheap.

A strong advocate for a less expensive route–seeking help from local colleges—is John McFarland, marketing services director for the Biloxi (Miss.) Sun and Herald. "Especially for smaller newspapers," McFarland said, "using local academic institutions is usually less expensive than professional survey firms. The results will probably be far more reliable than if you'd done it yourself, and the institutions are usually eager to take on such a project for the additional revenue and the chance to give students some practical experience."

Another example of such an arrangement was described by David G. Peters, city editor of the St. Cloud (Minn.) Daily Times, an afternoon paper with a circulation of 27,500. The Daily Times would not conduct polls, Peters said, without the existence of a research center at St. John's University in nearby Collegeville. The private liberal arts university includes a Center for Human and Community Development that Peters said is well-respected for its research, primarily into problems faced by small local governments.

"We contract with the center to conduct a monthly poll, asking enough questions that we have a story every Monday. The center is under faculty supervision but the actual telephoning is done by students. The center compiles the results, runs cross tabulations for age, sex, education, etc., and types the results up in a booklet delivered to us each month. We pay $100 a month for this. The questions are determined in a monthly session including the students conducting the poll, editors, one or more reporters and often a faculty adviser from the center. . . . The sample is selected by use of a table for random numbers, which designate a page of the telephone book for St. Cloud and the name to be used on that page."

This is a quantum jump over those polls on the price of oil and Sunday shopping hours. But professional survey people could find cause for criticism even in St. Cloud. They could challenge, for instance, the use of students as pollsters. Quality of interviewing is critical to the accuracy of a poll. So are many aspects of this complex means of research.

Another way of saying it is that polls are highly susceptible to distortion, which is all the more reason why people in the news business should treat them with a great deal more care.

When is a crowd really a multitude or more correctly a simple gathering? Crowd counting is an especially important art to political reporters or reviewers of rock concerts. Hype prevails in both of these types of stories as the aides of candidates and the road managers of rock stars are eager to add several thousands—or hundred thousands—to the number reported in the story. The police can often help bring such numbers to more rational levels, of course, but it is best done by reporters themselves. This December 1979 piece by the editors of *The Quill* tells how the *Chicago Tribune* estimated crowds during the 1979 visit of Pope John Paul II.

CROWD COUNTING: THERE'S MORE (CORRECTION, LESS) TO IT THAN MEETS THE EYE

The pope's coming to America (in 1979) was spectacular. The pope's coming to Chicago was even more special to the people of Chicago.

The visit of Pope John Paul II to the Second City was important for two reasons: the Chicago area is the largest Roman Catholic archdiocese in the nation, and Chicago boasts the second largest Polish population in the world, outside Warsaw.

For this man, there would be crowds in Chicago. They waited for him, in the cold, in the dark, along a stretch of Milwaukee Avenue in the heart of the city's Polish community as his motorcade sped past on his arrival. They jammed the grounds at Five Holy Martyrs Church in another section of the city where he celebrated Mass in Polish.

Officials were sure that the climactic event of the pope's visit to Chicago, the Mass at Grant Park on the city's lakefront, would draw the largest crowds. City officials were predicting more than one million people would show up.

The day of the afternoon Mass, Oct. 5, people started gathering early in the morning. Throughout the day, the pilgrimage continued.

Groups had lined Michigan Avenue, too, to watch the pope's motorcade proceed to the Mass site. When the pope passed by, at about 3:30 p.m., the people followed him to Grant Park. Then the Mass began.

Most network and local Chicago newscasts showed pictures of the crowd that had assembled—taken from the vantage point of the pope's altar, looking north. That view showed person next to person next to person . . . extending as far as the wall of skyscrapers in the background would allow. The sight was an impressive one.

But those who watched the pope's Mass from that wall of downtown commercial buildings and lakefront condominiums saw another sight—that of open green areas; people standing comfortably, not clustered tightly.

Police officials were estimating the crowd at more than one million. Those watching the proceedings from the city buildings probably didn't believe that estimate.

In fact, throughout the afternoon, officials supplied reporters with crowd figures that ranged from 500,000 to 1.75 million.

A police official admitted later that the crowd did not come close to the million figure police provided on the day of the Mass (and duly reported by the press); but since Philadelphia had claimed more than one million attended the pope's Mass there, the Chicago police official said, Chicago just couldn't come in second.

Following the wide range of official crowd counts, possibly all inflated, the Chicago Tribune set out to learn how many people did attend the Grant Park Mass—and how to count crowds.

The Tribune contacted four teams of government photo intelligence experts who examined Tribune photographers' shots of the Grant Park crowd. The figures were all different, and all much more conservative than those of the Chicago officials.

The largest estimate came from a group who calculated the number of persons who could stand shoulder to shoulder in the area taken up by the crowd. The team arrived at a figure of 350,000. Another team of experts studied the numbers of persons it could count from a series of Tribune photos. Its crowd estimate was the lowest—only 65,000.

The Tribune also sought the opinion of Maj. James Lindsay, commissioner of inspection for the Federal Park Police in Washington, D.C. Lindsay has been estimating the sizes of crowds in the mall around the Washington Monument for 11 years. Lindsay, who said he is "always generous and very conservative with my calculations of crowds," estimated the Grant Park gathering at no more than 100,000.

"I'm not interested in getting into an argument with Chicago police. But there is no way they could have had anywhere near a million people there," Lindsay said.

The commissioner of the Federal Park Police noted that most groups that rally at the Washington Monument are political, "and estimates of large crowds are self-serving. We are constantly catching hell from political groups. But I will stand by my figures."

Chicago officials continue to stand by their figures, too. Mayor Jane Byrne's press aide, Michael Sneed, who joined the administration just recently after leaving the Chicago Tribune as an investigative reporter, contended that the million count still held, but that there were "definitely no less than 800,000." She said she arrived at those figures by calculating the number of people who could fit into the "papal Mass area."

Tribune photographs showed the crowd covered an area of no more than 882,450 square feet. Photographs also showed the average density to be less than one person per six feet. With that formula, one group of experts questioned by the paper said no more than 167,000 persons could have attended the Mass.

"Who, what, when, where, why."

This litany fills the air on the first few days in any basic journalism class. But what of a sixth "W," "so what?" John Dart, a reporter for the Los Angeles *Times,* advocates its use in this May 1970 article as a way to improve the news gathering process itself. Dart says the device can be effective with one or two sentences of background followed by the latest developments to bring out the significance of an event and to enhance reader understanding of it. He thinks the inclusion of the "so what" angles will also increase readability— and may even add to the chances a story will be read at all.

THE SIXTH W—'SO WHAT?'

John Dart

Learning the 5 W's (what, who, when, where, why and sometimes how) was like learning to spell cat.

They were easy to learn, soon became second nature and we probably knew them before they were formally taught to us anyway.

A sixth question needs to be answered by most news stories—and isn't so easily remembered. That question is, "So what?" (Maybe comic book punctuation—"So what?!?"—is better because of its challenging, sometimes cynical nature.)

Asking the 6th W can be one of the most important considerations in the stages of news gathering—interviewing, writing and editing. The "so what of it" is assuredly on the minds of the typically hurried reader or impatient television viewer.

Obituaries are good examples. "Joe Doakes is dead. So what?" The who, what, when, where and why are obituary elements, but the so-what determines whether the story is written, and if so, what length and where it fits in the news report.

Some newsmen probably have this so-what guard against banality built into their writing-editing systems and have no need to reflect on it. I confess I have to remind myself to submit my own story ideas and stories to that question. Ever find yourself explaining to an editor (or to a reader or viewer, or to your unimpressed wife) why you think the story you wrote was significant? And then realizing that you could have included your indignant explanation in your story by use of more background information, quotes or other means?

Or does the editor or deskman later realize he could have brought home the significance of that wire story with the local impact in parentheses or in a sidebar?

The ways to answer "so what" are many. It mght be the unexpected elements of the event, the contrasts or apparent contrasts, the unusualness, the conclusiveness or inconclusiveness of it, the number of people affected or the probable impact on events to come.

An effective device used particularly on television news is to give one or two sentences of background, then tell the latest development to bring out the event's significance as well as make it understandable.

Asking the question "so what?" also should contribute to the trimming down or passing over some stories that don't stand up to the challenge. This shouldn't mean the light, the sad or the fun-to-read stories come out losers. The so-what-of-it here hopefully could be answered by the hints of humor, tension, irony or tragedy to come as you unfold the story.

For major stories, often stories involving physical action (space adventures, war actions, assassinations), the rapid and accurate assembling of facts in a lucid manner is the prime consideration. Little so-what bolstering is needed. The so-what angle usually comes out in later stories or in sidebars.

The action events that are obviously less important require more so-what challenging to put the story in perspective. Ignoring readers/ viewers who feel relating "bad" news encourages "bad" events, newsmen must neither give superficial treatment to protests nor play into the hands of dissident organizers who see the press as a tool. Asking "so what" until it hurts in this area and in other action stories—particularly crimes—should help cut down on news play that merely follows journalistic tradition on protests, murders, arsons, accidents, etc.

What concerns me especially are stories of significant developments that don't grab at your attention because they lack physical action or obvious drama.

One way to try for that attention is to include superlatives such as first, biggest, lowest, most dramatic—when these adjectives can be substantiated. I suspect that otherwise conscientious newsmen sometimes pass up chances to add that element to their stories. Calls for the modern news media to be more reflective and analytic in their approach does not mean all the superlatives have to be junked, associated as they are with a sensationalistic past in journalism. The superlatives help give perspective to the news consumer who isn't knowledgeable in the subject.

While establishing the significance of your news story in its particulars, you can also apply "so what" to the credibility of your article as a whole. You may have great quotes from a clergyman who wants to make radical changes, but it doesn't mean much in many cases unless that churchman is in a position of influence or he articulates broadly-felt attitudinal changes

Much of the news is news because it represents change or new problems. When changes and problems appear to proliferate in society many of the old guidelines for what is newsworthy are questioned? Just as "established" values in society are questioned. With such a broad range of opinions and supposed priorities in today's society, it's not surprising that any one person or organization would push any point of view. But it may be news if other groups are moving in the same direction.

The story based on one interview diminishes in importance in such times unless that interviewed person is particularly knowledgeable or influential. The balance is swinging, I think, to the round-up, trend and other multi-source stories, which lend themselves to more credibility as well as more significance.

There was a time when it was said that of all the five W's, "why" was the most important element. This was because of the stated need for in-depth reporting. I would object to continuing, consciously or subconsciously, this orientation in interpretive news. If you launch right into your well-researched, 3,000-word thesis on why something is happening or happened, you may be eliminating a lot of the audience if you neglect the so-what-of-it.

Some readers/viewers are aware, for instance, that there have been some apparently significant developments in that country or that branch of science or on the college campuses. But they have not had the desire to really delve into it or build up their understanding as the news developed. Many would take the time for a story that has a so-what thrust, I believe, in spite of its length. Telling "why" or "how" works best when the import is known, and only the why or how of it has been untold.

The public perhaps is becoming accustomed to the documentary or in-depth interpretive story as a delayed way to find out "what it all means." But that shouldn't excuse writers and editors working on the daily news report from asking and answering the question "so what?" as much as time, accuracy and fairness will allow.

Allowing a source to read a story before publication is a practice that engenders mixed feelings from reporters and editors. In some technical reporting areas like science, it *is* sometimes advantageous to let sources read a finished story for accuracy. Errors can be corrected easily, thus preserving the credibility of reporters and their scientist / sources who are forever worried that their peers will think badly of them for talking to a journalist in the first place.

That's the up side of the argument. On the down side is the fact that few people can stick to merely correcting errors. Give sources the chance to look at what they said—and what the reporter wrote— and before long they are changing everything. In this May 1973 article, James W. Tankard Jr. of the University of Texas at Austin and Michael Ryan, now at West Virginia University, review the results of their survey on this subject, citing the pros and cons of review.

THE RIGHT OF REVIEW: ERROR CHECK OR CENSORSHIP?

James W. Tankard, Jr.
and
Michael Ryan

Should news sources, particularly in specialized areas such as science, be permitted to review the accuracy of articles about their work before publication? This is a question expected to become increasingly controversial in the next few years.

A number of writers has suggested that newspapers need to shift their focus from general spot news coverage to in-depth reporting of science, economics, urban problems, mental health, environment and other specialized areas. As more reporting is done on these complex topics, the requests by sources for a "right of review" are likely to increase. And there are signs that submitting articles to sources might become an issue in general reporting as well.

The traditional argument against prior review by the source is described in William Rivers' "Free-Lancer and Staff Writer" by a writer for *Ski* magazine:

At some magazines, checking copies of articles are sent to all sources and to all people involved in the article. At Ski, showing copy to any outsider is strictly forbidden. Bill Berry, the executive editor, commented, "Nothing can compromise the integrity of a magazine more quickly than this."

Former *Saturday Review* science editor John Lear expressed in *Columbia Journalism Review* his criticism of scientists who want to review his copy:

> I cleary remember the cries of pain and rage that rose in the scientific community after the early issues of Saturday Review's Science and Humanity Supplement. That any layman would dare to write about scientists and their experiments without submitting his copy to them for editing (no one would admit it was censorship) in advance of publication! . . . . I cannot recall how long it has been since a scientist tried to bludgeon me into submitting my copy to him. The gambit now is more wary, taking some such form as "I'll be happy to help you check your story before you print it." I gather from the persistence of such approaches that at least some other science writers are dutifully submitting copy and accepting whatever revisions are handed out.

Unlike Lear, other journalists have been willing to grant a right of review, particularly in cases where they needed to do so to obtain their stories.

Some highly respected reporters made such an arrangement with Aflred Kinsey in order to see galley proofs of "Sexual Behavior in the Human Female." A Ph.D. dissertation at Indiana University by Del Brinkman points out that journalists were allowed to do prepublication stories on the Kinsey book only if they signed a three-page agreement and traveled personally to the university at Bloomington to be briefed on the book. The agreement required each writer to limit his story to 5,000 words and then submit the story to Kinsey for correction of factual errors. About 60 journalists, including Alton Blakeslee of the Associated Press, Ernest Havemann of *Life,* Boyd Gill of United Press, Earl Ubell of the New York *Herald Tribune* and Pierre C. Fraley of the Philadelphia *Bulletin,* agreed to come on these terms. Brinkman states that if there were any objections to the three-page agreement they were mild ones and came primarily from the wire services.

Kinsey spent much of his time in July and August, 1953, checking articles for accuracy. We asked Fraley about this, and he told us, "He (Kinsey) could make other suggestions for change, but the reporter would not be obligated to take those suggestions."

Fraley, than president of the Council for the Advancement of Science Writing, said in our interview with him that he is against a blanket policy of permitting sources to review copy. But he conceded, "Science news often is very complex and technical, and for that reason the need for review may be a bit greater than for other kinds of news."

We found evidence of the need for source review of science articles in a recent survey on the accuracy of science news. The general technique of the study was to send clippings of science articles with accuracy questionnaires to scientists quoted as principal sources in the articles. We sent out 242 questionnaires and received 193 replies, for a response rate of 79.8 per cent. Scientists were invited to write comments on the questionnaires, and more than half did. The most frequent comment (mentioned by more than 10 per cent of those who wrote comments) was that scientists should be permitted to review articles on their work before publication.

The study also uncovered at least two cases in which an accuracy check by a source would have prevented ill-fated consequences for scientists.

One case involved a wire service story describing a program of research on the disease, polycythemia vera. The clipping mailed in the study bore the headline, "Blood, Bone Cancer Possibly Controlled." The complete article read:

> Doctors at _____ College of Medicine say they have controlled a form of cancer of the blood and bone marrow by removing Vitamin B2 from patients' diets.
> Dr. _____ , professor of pharmacology and medicine, said Monday that patients deprived of the vitamin had not showed signs of the disease, polycythemia vera, for up to four years.
> _____ added, however, the disease was a slow cancer that may take years to kill, and it is too early to say the experiment is a cure. He also said other treatments had arrested the disease for the same length of time, but it eventually reappeared.
> Vitamin B2, also called riboflavin, is found in milk, meat, and most prepared foods.

The doctor who was quoted stated on his questionnaire that the lead and headline were imprecise and misleading. He added: "(The word) 'cure' should never have been used in this article at all, even if prefaced by 'too early to say,' since unfortunate victims of cancer focus on this word."

The scientist described problems the inaccurate reporting created for him: "Hundreds of letters, phone calls and telegrams (were) received as a result of the original article, this condensation, and inaccurate . . . wire releases—the majority of which were from patients (or relatives) with diseases other than polycythemia vera."

Finally, the researcher commented on the need for a review by the scientist:

> Over 1 1/2 hours (were) spent with this reporter, carefully explaining the work, its preliminary nature, the need for conservative reporting and for accuracy. There was no urgency to "meet a deadline." The reporter was specifically requested to allow me to review the report for accuracy, etc., prior to printing, but this was denied on the grounds that it would interfere with "freedom of the press."

OUR SURVEY revealed another case of inaccurate reporting of medical information, this one involving work on a treatment for psoriasis. In this case, newsmen were given a press release describing the research, but problems arose when it was rewritten.

The headline of this story read, "Psoriasis Cure Breakthrough Seen." The lead of a wire service story read: "University of _____ scientists Wednesday announced a breakthrough in treating psoriasis, the skin disease which causes misery for about 6 million Americans."

The project director expressed dismay on his questionnaire at the use of the words "cure" and "breakthrough":

> We prepared a carefully written story for _____ news information service. Nowhere in that write-up nor at the meeting was the word breakthrough used. (The) last sentence of our write-up said cure of psoriasis is probably 50 years away. Yet the title of this article you sent says "Psoriasis Cure Breakthrough Seen." All I can say is, for Christ's sake!

The scientist added that the press coverage caused him to receive several thousand letters that he was not able to answer. "I have the phone ringing every 5 to 10 minutes with patients from all over the world," he said.

This case points out the difficulty of insuring accuracy in science reporting, since the news stories were based on a press release and not on interviews. Even with a press release, serious distortions can occur.

A vertebrate zoologist contacted through our study summarized the scientists' arguments for a right of review:

> I would think at least 95 per cent of scientists' complaints about the published versions of their own story to a reporter could probably be eliminted by allowing the interviewed scientist to read and edit as necessary the final story copy before printing—although I fully realize this would very seldom be practical. However, just having the reporter read his version to the scientist—and incorporating any essential corrections and additions—before submission of the story to the editorial staff would often be practical. And, this would certainly lead to a better relationship between scientist and reporter—with the general public being the beneficiary.

The principal argument for a right of review by the source is to achieve the highest possible accuracy in reporting. This is the argument that led Hugh C. Sherwood to conclude in his recent book, "The Journalistic Interview," that "the case for checking out articles is much stronger than the case against it."

Carrying this position to its extreme would be to allow review of an entire article with the understanding that all recommended changes will be made. In other words, the source is given final editorial decision power over what will appear in an article. This kind of pre-publication review appears to be common with news bureaus or public relations offices, which are in the position of being employed by the people they are writing about. Scientists at universities and scientific institutions are often given the opportunity to rewrite news releases before they are sent out. However, similar right of full review is sometime given by news reporters when it is the only way they can get an exclusive story. For instance, a scientist in our study—a researcher in psychiatry —said he gave a story to a wire service reporter "as a news break" and then "supervised" the final story.

THEN WHAT are the reasons for not allowing sources to review stories?

• There often is not time to allow a source to review an article before a deadline. This argument applies principally to news stories and less to magazine articles or newspaper features.

• A source may not be able to rise above his own self-interest enough to comment only on factual errors. A source, influenced by his own involvement in a story, can drift easily into criticism of the reporter's interpretations, news judgment and style.

• A reporter cannot always guarantee that changes suggested by a source will indeed be made. Articles go through an editorial process involving a number of decision-makers, and the reporter himself usually does not have the final authority.

• The source may be responsible for only a part of an article, while the writer is responsible for the entire article. If there are inaccuracies, the writer is the one who ultimately must take the blame. Therefore, the final word on what goes in article or how it is written should rest with the writer.

• Some writers, such as John Lear, apparently consider any kind of source review as censorship and a threat to freedom of the press. These writers argue that if a right of review is extended to a Nobel Prize-winning scientist, it could then be demanded by any newsmaker, such as a party to an automobile accident.

• A source who doesn't like an article he reviews may take steps to keep it from being printed. Pierre Fraley mentions the possibilities of a source going to a publisher to halt publication, or of a source going to the competition to give them a scoop.

Most newsmen at present apparently do not permit a source review of any type. Prof. Jim R. Morris of Kansas State University reported in a recent paper that 87 per cent of the reporters responding to a survey on interviewing did not permit any source editing at all.

The alternatives for the journalist, however, do not necessarily have to be limited to a choice between no review and giving the source the final word. A right of review can be extended at least two other ways:

• *Partial review.* The source is given access to selected material from the article, such as quotations, figures or analogies, and is asked to verify its accuracy. Many magazines are now using this kind of prepublication review.

For instance, Gene Bylinsky, a staff writer for *Fortune,* describes in Rivers' book the processing of a staff-written manuscript. After the managing editor approves a second draft, Bylinsky says, a process of "closing" takes place. One part of this process is that the manuscript is checked by a researcher, who calls sources to check on quotations, figures, etc.

   • *Review to suggest changes.* The source is given access to the entire article and is asked to point out factual errors and suggest other changes, but the understanding is that the reporter and his editors have the final word. This was the kind of review that writers granted to Kinsey when they signed the three-page agreement. It is apparently being used now by some science writers, as the following account by a zoologist in our survey indicates:

> (The reporter) spent almost two hours interviewing me in my lab in getting the story. Then, by coincidence, when I happened to phone him on another matter late that afternoon, he was just about to turn in the completed story and asked me if he could read it to me to check for accuracy. Happily, I had only one or two almost insignificant corrections to make—which he was most happy to incorporate.

Both of the above intermediate positions combine the advantages of improving accuracy of reporting and keeping the final editorial decision with the reporter and his editors.

Pierre Fraley points out that the decision of whether or not to permit a source review is influenced by the kind of relationship that exists between reporter and source.

"There has got to be some kind of mutual trust between the writer and the source," he said. "If the source is acting as a censor, we don't want that. He's got to understand some of the problems facing the reporter."

Fraley argues that science writing differs from some other kinds of reporting in that the source is not interested in withholding information from the public. He says that both the scientist and the reporter are dedicated to a common problem—communicating difficult information to the public. "If there is an adversary relationship, then you've got a problem."

Even with the prevalent use of tape recorders in journalism, a wise reporter still takes notes. This notetaking, in handwriting that ranges from that of a doctor on a prescription blank to an Egyptian scribe proficient in hieroglyphics, takes a number of forms. In December 1980, Hiley Ward, a Temple University journalism professor, took a random survey of reporters around the country to determine how they take their notes and what they write on. He follows this amusing collection of opinions with his own suggestions of abbreviations to speed the often grueling process of writing down in a hurry what sources are saying at a pace that would make an auctioneer blink.

ON TAKING NOTES: OFF THE CUFF

Hiley H. Ward

Reporters will write on anything and everything, from typing paper folded in half to the backs of checks and martini napkins. And they are equally resourceful when it comes to actually taking down information. For instance:

One investigative reporter from Newsday says he never uses the standard reporter's notebook: "Too bulky, a turnoff to witnesses."

Barbara Herrera, of the San Diego Tribune, prefers yellow legal pads.

"Pocket-size cards," says a San Diego Union reporter. Margins of handouts, adds a New York Times reporter.

Martha Shirk, of the St. Louis Post-Dispatch, sometimes writes on whatever scraps of paper are in her purse: credit card receipts, envelopes, gum wrappers, paycheck stubs. "It's often quite embarrassing, but it only happens when I find a story by chance, a murder on the way home from work, for instance!"

Skip Hess, of the Indianapolis News, says he has made use of grocery sacks.

Then, there's the procedure that borders on the absurd. Robert Strauss, of the Philadelphia Daily News, remembers:

"One guy used to write notes on his arm. . . . One time he took off his shirt and went down his side . . . don't know whether he ever got confused with his tatoo."

On notetaking, reporters say:

"Paraphrase and put quote marks around the 'most important' words or phrases."—Tyree Johnson, Philadelphia Daily News.

"Listen for key phrases and do not try for extended verbatim notes."—Edward Cowan, New York Times.

"Take it down word for word in Gregg shorthand."—Barbara Herrera, San Diego Tribune.

"Use combintaion of shortened words (as long as they'll be understood exactly), abbreviations, and shorthand."—Samuel L. Singer, Philadelphia Inquirier.

"Write slowly and use large, distinct characters."—Jeff Williamson, Wichita Eagle-Beacon.

"Mentally memorize each statement and try as quickly as possible to get it down."—Roxi Mueller, Fort Wayne (Ind.) Journal-Gazette.

Anonymous Suggestions

Put down only the first letter of every word, and spell out key words, or about every fifth or sixth word, as time permits—then immediately go back over this key paragraph, and fill out all of the words—as the press conference or broadcast continues.

To avoid confusing speakers: Assign each peson in your notes a number, accompanied in the first reference in the notes by a two-word description: e.g., number 1, bald, checkered shirt; 2, blonde, striped blouse, etc. Then afterwards, corner the participant or speaker for his or her name, and take the person's name down with the corresponding number.

Unusual, but smart, is the reporter who uses colored pencils. Blue for Smith, red for Jones, green for Williams and so on.

Draw a line across the page after each speaker concludes, thus clearly separating his remarks from another's.

When You Have Questions

"My only symbol is to put a question mark in parentheses after words I doubt, or to bracket a passage that needs further amplification."—Jeff Williamson, Wichita Eagle-Beacon.

"I draw a box around such information."—Ray Ruppert, Seattle Times.

"Circle a word for spelling; put question mark beside information to be checked."—Jan Schaffer, federal courthouse reporter for the Philadelphia Inquirer.

"As? means to check it out; Sp? means to check the spelling."—Carol Green, Denver Post.

"A CQ? for check later."—George Skelton, Sacramento bureau chief, Los Angeles Times.

"CK for check out a fact with a certain authority."—Constance Y. Bramson, lifestyle editor, Harrisburg Patriot-Evening News. (Also some use "ch" after anything that needs to be checked.)

Certainly all of this advice would be useful to the Minnesota newsman who confided:

"I take notes poorly. Occasionally I have seen the notes of others here in the office. They always seem more legible and more complete than mine. I wonder how I survive!"

How to Speed Up Taking Notes

ausa—assistant U.S. attorney
bg—background
bk—book
cgx—Congress
cr—classroom
c/r—courtroom
ctrm—courtroom
cty—city
da—district attorney
enuf—enough
est—establish
f—father
fed—federal
g—guard
gg—going
hpnd—happened
invu—interview
j—judge
l—lawyer
m—mayor; mother
nfa—not for attribution
o/c—organized crime

OR—off record
pple—people
px—police
rdi—ready
rep—representative
sap—soon as possible
sch—school
sitn—situation
std—standard
th—that or there
TO—turnover
trsy—treasury
u/—under (u/stndg—understanding)
u r—you are
viz.—namely
w/—with
w/o—without
wt–what
xgr—legislature
Xn—Christian (Xnty—Christianity)
y p—young people

—Hiley Ward

When does a quote cease to be a quote and become a reporter's version of what a source said? The difficulty of getting everything down exactly as stated in an interview is a journalistic problem of longstanding. Handling direct quotations properly is a crucial part of press credibility. As with so much of our beloved profession, luck plays as much a part in this process as skill.

News organizations have policies for dealing with direct quotations as a December 1980 survey by L. Dupre Long of Memphis State University reviews.

Sometimes, however, the most experienced reporter can get into trouble over the handling of quotes. In 1980, Wayne Thompson, a reporter for the Portland *Oregonian,* gained national notoriety over the quotes of then Washington governor Dixy Lee Ray he used in a story. Thompson explained what happened at a local SPJ, SDX chapter meeting as reported here by Ron Lovell, an Oregon State journalism professor.

IN QUOTATION, LET ME SAY . . .

L. Dupre Long

Early fall (of 1980) reporter Wayne Thompson was suspended from the Portland Oregonian payroll for fabricating quotes attributed to outgoing Gov. Dixy Lee Ray. In defense, Thompson said he was forced to rely on sketchy notes from the interview because his tape recorder malfunctioned. Mechanical failure did not exonerate him. Apparently his editors were not swayed, it being their philosophy that if you are not sure about a quote you had better check with the speaker.

The Thompson case was probably viewed by reporters everywhere with a varying range of emotions, although many of them must have thought, "There but for the grace of God go I." A survey done shortly before the suspension found reporters who admitted to making up and doctoring quotes, and many papers without formal policies—policies that could forestall what happened to Thompson.

"I do occasionally reconstruct from memory," said a Wall Street Journal reporter.

A Memphis reporter explained that one of his best sources curses constantly and that if he didn't clean up the language he would soon be looking for a job with another newspaper.

Others reported that news sources, in spontaneous interviews, do not speak coherently enough to be quoted directly.

"If you are dead sure that you know what a person is saying and if that person is suffering from the sort of glottal paralysis which renders his every expressed thought an inchoate, incoherent thing, then smoothing out his quote is a mercy not a mischief," according to one Miami Herald reporter.

". . . Clarity should be the canon. If a source meanders on and on you simply have to take a knife somewhere and pick out the salient aspects of what he's saying.

". . . It's a tricky business though, and requires a lot of judgment."

An editor of a highly respected Midwest newspaper where there are no "hard and fast" rules agrees: "Good sense is still the best policy."

Houston Chronicle Managing Editor Don Pickels answered, "Yes, we clean up grammar and syntax when it is obvious the speaker has more than a nodding acquaintance with the English language. Also we avoid quoting dialect for the most part (we're goona do this or that). Otherwise we would play hell quoting President Carter—or just about anyone—with fidelity. We don't have enough apostrophes to handle all the runnin' and funnin' and sunnin' that goes on in the Sunbelt. I believe after cleansing the grammar and syntax that we do a pretty good job with direct quotes."

The Philadelphia Inquirer has a written policy, although it is oriented more toward copy editors than reporters. It reads:

"Generally direct quotations are not altered in the editing process. However, we repair minor grammatical errors in direct quotations unless those errors are pertinent to the news—or are deemed to be extremely important in reporting color. We should fix such minor errors especially in cases when they might take on undue importance and cause the speaker to look foolish. However, we would not change a quotation simply because of an error in agreement with an antecedent, for example, since such errors are accepted in colloquial speech. Mispronunciations, such as gonna for going to, are corrected, as they are acceptable to common speech but make a speaker appear to be inarticulate when rendered in writing. The use of the parenthetical "sic" is limited to instances in which the reader might be unable to discern whether a conscious error had been committed. Quoting in dialect may be done only rarely and must be in good taste."

To avoid problems, Dallas Morning News City Editor Don Smith says: "Quotations should be used sparingly; you are writing a news or feature story, not transcribing a conversation. . . . For the most part, paraphrase. Use a direct quote only when the person being quoted has something to say that merits a quote. Do not interpret what the person is saying and then put that interpretation in quotes."

In the long run, reporters see the test as fidelity to meaning and intent, not to stenographic exactitude. Luckily, that seems to be the prevailing attitude among editors, too.

WRONG WAY STRETCH: SCOOPS VANISH, CREDIBILITY REMAINS—AS ONE REPORTER LEARNED AFTER RE-CREATING QUOTES.

Ron Lovell

In September 1980, Wayne Thompson, a longtime reporter and editorial writer for the Portland *Oregonian,* obtained an exclusive interview with Washington Gov. Dixy Lee Ray, the first after her defeat in the primary election. Thompson conducted the interview succesfully enough but discovered later that night at the office that his tape recorder had malfunctioned and he could not decipher all of what she had said. Thompson prepared the interview material anyway. The newspaper had promoted the two articles he wrote and was planning to use color photographs of the governor. The reporter did not tell his editors of his troubles with the tape or that he had reconstructed some of the governor's comments and used them as direct quotes.

Some weeks later, Gov. Ray charged fabrication after she had reviewed her own tapes of the interview. The *Oregonian* ran a retraction and suspended Thompson without pay for eight weeks.

In 1981, Thompson talked about his interview at a meeting of the SPJ,SDX Willamette Valley professional chapter in Portland. Because this incident and his remarks bear on the subject of credibility, they constitute a useful sidelight to the Janet Cooke affair.

"There's nothing about the Dixy Lee Ray incident to applaud. In my view it was a low level example of journalism that should not be condoned or excused, not by anyone . . . and not by me. I will offer no excuses or arguments to defend my performance on the night of Sept. 19 (1980). I will try to shed some light on how, with the benefit of hindsight, I allowed myself to blunder so badly. . . .

"I'd like to discuss another pivotal subject on this matter, it's credibility. I have long held that credibility is the most precious commodity that we in the communications media have to sell. Without it, readers and viewers will not believe what we're trying to tell them. We're just peddling a lot of words without credibility. When a newspaper, TV station or magazine does a credible job in reporting a news story, the impact rubs off favorably on the rest of us. Readers are not all that byline conscious. If a colleague does a good job, I can feel good about it. Conversely, a bad journalistic effort like the one I created on Sept. 19 rubs off on every working journalist. . . .

"The assignment came to me in a rather natural way. When Gov. Ray lost the election, the managing editor asked me to make an attempt to call her to see if we could get an interview with her. I was willing to try. My relationship with the governor in the past has been an unusual, even an unhealthy one. I had some confidence, if I put my request in, somehow we would get that opportunity."

Thompson says his confidence was based on the fact that he had interviewed her prior to this incident and helped her prepare a series of articles on nuclear power in 1975 before she ran for governor.

"Gov. Ray didn't have a secretary or staff (in 1975) but was very willing to talk, not so willing to put it in journalistic style. That became my task. Now I question this as a healthy arrangement. In going over that series (now) I recognize some of my words, arguments, synonyms and metaphors. I read the (1975) story to her on the phone and she accepted a lot of the things I had done. . . . It spawned a closer reporter/source relationship than is healthy. Because the reporter/source realtionship began with my putting words in her mouth for a six-part series, I suspect that red warning signals did not go up Sept. 19 when I (put) the piece together from fragmentary notes into full direct quotes. . . . Subconsciously I gave myself license and permission to attempt total recall of what she said because she had accepted my words in the past.

"Since that '75 series, my relationship has been arms length for me, but trusting from her." Thompson interviewed her after her election in 1976 and at other times in the years since. Ironically, he turned down the latest chance to interview her during his suspension period. "She called me at home to offer her support. She said she planned no interviews with reporters but would leave office quietly. 'If your paper approves and you want to come up, I will grant you another exclusive interview during the transition,' she said. I told the governor I appreciated her having trust in me but I wouldn't want to do it. I didn't tell her what I was really thinking: Governor, I wouldn't touch that interview with a 10-foot pole, your tape recorder or mine."

For the September interview, Thompson drove to Olympia accompanied by a photographer for his 3 p.m. appointment with Gov. Ray. "I didn't feel particularly tired or worn out. I was functioning fairly well. I went into the room, greeted the governor and set up my tape recorder on the desk. I got my notebook out. She had a press aide in the room. The interview was not an interview any reporter would want to adopt as a style. I had known her long enough that our discussions were conversational. I asked her several questions but in such a way that I would make a statement and she would respond. Part of that technique is not reportorial but editorial. . . . The interview lasted for a little over an hour. . . . She had a microphone on her tape recorder— one of those reel-to-reel jobs. I got feedback that gave me a high pitched hum that ran through my tapes. What that did for me or didn't do for me, it meant I could hear some of what she said—some of her statements—before her voice would trail off at the end. I could hear a lot of what I'd said. Other parts of the tape I couldn't hear myself or her. I heard enough, it appeared, to tease me into making the attempt (to reconstruct the quotes).

"There were 15 quotes in two stories that were precisely accurate. These were ones I transcribed, that I could hear everything. . . .These became the entrapment quotes. Because I had them it gave me false confidence to pursue the ones that weren't full direct quotes. In retracting the story, 20 quotes in some way—major or minor—were off-base, 9 were labeled by Gov. Ray's press secretary as fabrications. I had 17 pages of notes in all. All but two quotes the governor's press aide claimed were fabricated came from my notebook or from part of the tape I could make out—phrases I scribbled in my notebook to try to remember. I blew it badly. My mind played tricks on me. In 26 years in this business, my memory of what people say to me rarely, if ever, betrayed me. One of the frustrating things about this—using my memory of a state-ment as nearly close to the precise statement that I will get in the tape re-corder. The fact that it didn't is very bothersome. The irony in all this: if there had been nothing to hear on that tape, a total malfunction, I would probably have given in to the good judgment of chucking the whole thing, putting it off until I could retrieve the governor's tape. The interview would have still been exclusive for us. My biggest error in judgment is not recognizing my notes and tapes were so incomplete that I would not risk doing the story. But the mix of some precise transcribed material that produced accurate quotes and fragmentary notes which destroyed me served to entice me to ignore the good judgment and pursue the effort. . . ."

Thompson first knew he had a problem with the interview when he got a letter from the governor on Oct. 6. In it she mentioned the errors and asked him why he had done it. He was shocked at the problems and tried to call her, reaching a press aide instead. The aide said she was upset "by a couple of quotes, it's not a big deal." Thompson says the aide gave him the impression not to worry.

On Oct. 10, he received a formal letter of complaint, the transcript, a copy of his story with several quotes underlined and a comparison of the two versions, with his indicated as "inaccurate" and "fabricated." The governor did not make a formal request for retraction. Thompson says no lawyers were contacted on either side. The retraction was made and the action taken against Thompson soon afterward.

In the months since—both during his suspension and since his return to the *Oregonian*—Thompson has had a lot of time to think about what happened to him.

"Credibility is a very precious commodity. . . . It may not be as frequent as we think. The *Oregonian* improved its credibility by publishing a lengthy and complete retraction on Oct. 21. I'm proud of that precedent-setting decision, not just because my butt got saved but because I can take some pride of authorship in the solution. . . ."

He says he received fewer letters than he expected on the matter and most agreed that it was an honest mistake. Nor do his sources treat him any differently. He looks at things differently, however.

"I have not been in the past all that forgiving of faux pas . . . but . . . I've been taught some compassion, no doubt some overdue himility and the sense that people, unlike a wolf pack, do not descend on a . . . wounded member of the pack and devour him. The support I've received . . . I will never forget.

"The next time a reporter comes up to me and says, 'There but for the grace of God go I,' I'm going to say . . . 'Don't ever make this mistake. The road is full of potholes, dangerous intersections and crossroads that lead to nowhere in particular and worse, you'll be driving down that road the rest of your life, looking for the turn-off to serenity.'"

Beyond personal interviews, the reporting for any article often begins with reference books and library research. Experienced reporters have their own shelves of indispensable books. Michael Ryan of West Virginia University compiled a good one in March 1977.

THE EASIEST COURSE AS A MATTER OF SOURCE

Michael Ryan

Few journalists know offhand the meaning of the term "interlocutory order," the total value of new construction last year in the United States, or the name of the first person to go over Niagara Falls in a barrel. And it isn't necessary that they spend time learning such information.

It is important, however, that they know they can find definitions of legal terms in **Black's Law Dictionary,** facts about construction in the United States in **Statistical Abstract of the United States,** the "first person who . . ." in **Famous First Facts,** and countless other answers in dozens of other sources.

The following are just a few of the many important written sources with which journalists should be familiar:

The Almanac of American Politics
America Votes
American Medical Directory
Art Index
Ayer Directory of Publications
Bartlett's Familiar Quotations
Black's Law Dictionary
The Book of the States
Broadcasting Yearbook
Chamber's Biographical Directory
Congressional Quarterly Almanac
Congressional Quarterly Weekly Report
Congressional Record
Congressional Staff Directory
Contemporary Authors
County and City Data Book
Current Biography

This article first appeared in *Journalism Educator* and appears with the permission of the editor of that publication.

Directory of American Scholars
Editor & Publisher Year Book
Education Index
Facts on File
Famous First Facts
Federal Register
Guinness Book of World Records
Hammond Medallion World Atlas
Index to Current Urban Documents
Information Please Almanac, Atlas and Yearbook
International Bibliography, Information, Documentation
International Year Book and Statesmen's Who's Who
Man and the Environment: A Bibliography of Selected Publications of
        the United Nations System 1946–1971
Monthly Catalog of United States Government Publications
Monthly Checklist of State Publications
The Municipal Year Book
The New York Times Encyclopedic Almanac
The New York Times Index
Official Congressional Directory
The Oxford Dictionary of Quotations
Pocket Data Book: USA, 1973
Power and Research Reactors in Member States (from the United Na-
        tions' International Atomic Energy Agency)
Publications of the United Nations System: A Reference Guide
Rand McNally News Cosmopolitan World Atlas
Readers' Guide to Periodical Literature
Roget's International Thesaurus
Shepard's Citations
State "blue books" or almanacs
State of Food and Agriculture (from the United Nations Food and Ag-
        riculture Organization)
The Stateman's Year-Book
Statistical Abstact of the United States
UN Statistical Yearbook
UNESCO (United Nations Educational, Scientific and Cultural Organ-
        ization) **Statistical Yearbook**
United States Statutes at Large
United States Code Annotated
Vital Speeches of the Day
Washington Information Directory
Webster's Biographical Dictionary

Webster's Dictionary of Synonyms
Weekly Compilation of Presidential Documents
Who's Who in America (Marquis)
The World Almanac & Book of Facts
World Who's Who in Science
Yearbook of the United Nations

Some of the kinds of questions one might ask on a fairly uncomplicated reference exercise are:

• Who is the publisher of the Columbus (Ohio) Citizen-Journal? (Source: **Editor & Publisher Year Book**)

• Who is Gilbert Charles Bourne? (Source: **World Who's Who in Science**)

• What is double jeopardy? (Source: **Black's Law Dictionary**)

• What were the 10 largest cities (by population) in the United States in 1980? (Source: **The World Almanac & Book of Facts**)

• Who is the president of Zambia? (Source: **The Statesman's Yearbook**)

• How many daily, semiweekly, weekly and biweekly periodicals are published in the State of Oregon? (Source: **Ayer Directory of Publications**)

• Who is Bernice Elizabeth Kauffman? (Source: **Who's Who of American Women**)

• The United States Senate discussed on June 5, 1974, a proposal to extend the Anadromous Fish Conservation Act. What sort of extension (in years) was requested? (Source: **Congressional Record**)

• Who is Tom McCall? (Source: **Current Biography**)

• How many articles about documentary photography were published between March 1970 and February 1971? (Source: **Readers' Guide to Periodical Literature**)

• Who was James H. Fairchild? (Source: **Webster's Biographical Dictionary**)

• Who was the first aeronautical stowaway? (Source: **Famous First Facts**)

• What nation is located due west of Malaysia? (Source: **National Geographic Atlas of the World**)

• Who is Wilmot Adolphus David? (Source: **The International Who's Who**)

• How much money does the New York Times Magazine pay for full-length articles which it publishes? (Source: **Writer's Market '82**)

• Who said: "To make your children capable of honesty is the beginning of education"? (Source: **The Oxford Dictionary of Quotations**)

• Who is the state senator who represents the district in which you live? (Source: State "blue book" or almanac)

• Who represents the 3rd Congressional District of Rhode Island? (Source: **Official Congressional Directory**)

• How many persons are employed by the fire department in Brownwood, Texas? (Source: **The Municipal Year Book**)

• What did the Supreme Court of Appeals of West Virginia do in the case of *Anne R. Cox v. Ruth Cox Turner* (case number 13223) on April 30, 1974? (Source: **South Eastern Reporter**)

There are literally hundreds of written information sources which might be useful to the working journalist,

—City health department records on communicable diseases, birth and death records, laboratory food tests.

—License and inspection department records on building permits issued for new construction or changes in existing structures, water and sewer permits, licenses or permits issued for new restaurants and other facilities.

—Zoning board records on variances requested, variances approved, variances denied.

—Purchasing and inventory department records on new typewriters and other office supplies purchased, costs of new city equipment (e.g., fire trucks, police cars, road construction equipment), contracts between the city and private contractors.

—Briefs filed in court by plaintiffs and defendants, transcripts of old cases, cases docketed for the future.

Writing

When we have snared our reader with a sharp lead, have answered all of his main questions, have eliminated all ambiguity, and have not turned him off with bewilderingly long sentences—like this one—or puzzled him with questionable quotes, we must make sure we don't spoil everything by misspelling or misusing any words.

A report of the Writing/Editing
Committee of the Associated Press
Managing Editors Association

Bad habits begun early in a writer's career are often hard to break. A reporter who gets used to certain questionable approaches to writing often repeats the same mistakes over and over again in copy, usually without realizing it. The Associated Press Managing Editors Association has long had a Writing/Editing Committee to check wire copy for such reoccurring mistakes. In this October 1971 article, Orville E. Lomoe, then executive editor of the Duluth, Minnesota *Herald and News-Tribune,* tells how the committee works and what its members tear their collective hair about.

FRAGGING WITH A TYPEWRITER AND OTHER BAD HABITS

*'. . . why don't yer speak so as
I can understand yer?'*

Orville E. Lomoe

FRAGGING. Bad leads. Poor explanations. Bad grammar. Vogue words. Etc. Etc.

Seasoned editors keep watch over copy for errors and mistakes. They constantly analyze, criticize and occasionally praise the quality of writing that goes into their publications and over the airwaves.

One group of editors which scrutinizes wire copy is the Writing/Editing Committee of the Associated Press Managing Editors Association. In its reports this year (1971), the committee says some excellent work is being done. But the committee members have also found some new mistakes in addition to a lot of old ones.

Take, for example, what the report called fragging with a typewriter (not to be confused with the act of a soldier in Vietnam tossing a fragmentation grenade at his officer or non-com). "Fragging" with respect to wire copy is the act of putting one or two words in quotation marks. The result is called a partial or fragmentary quote.

"Many AP writers are guilty of this type of fragging. And the AP report is overloaded with fragmentary quotes because editors are not editing the fragging writers," the committee report said.

It is obvious that in most cases the quote marks are not needed. The quoted matter is properly attributed and the quotes add nothing. Quote marks also tend to give the reader the impression that the writer doesn't believe what is being said and puts quotes on the word or phrase to tell the reader, "This is what he said but we don't quite believe it."

One editor who gags at frags pointed out that editors can't always repair a partial quote: "Only the guy with the original notes can get the quote right."

Two examples:

"SANTIAGO—The biggest publishing house in Chile said Wednesday it is 'impossible' to pay government-ordered wage hikes. . . ."

"HAMILTON, Bermuda—The new year here started with an outbreak of what police described as 'spontaneous' vandalism."

THEN THERE is a somewhat sad commentary entitled "Word to the Wise." Says the report:

"When we have snared our reader with a sharp lead, have answered all of his main questions, have eliminated all ambiguity, and have not turned him off with bewilderingly long sentences—like this one—or puzzled him with questionable quotes, we must make sure we don't spoil everything by mis-spelling or misusing any words.

"We don't want to get smart-aleck letters to the editor saying:

" 'Don't you know that kidnap is not a noun?'

" 'Don't you know the difference between a nuclear rocket and a nuclear warhead?'

" 'Don't you know that protest against is redundant?' "

ANOTHER AREA which needs constant policing is lead writing. The committee found a wide range. Some good examples:

"HYDEN, KY.—'Some people say we ought to quit going in them mines,' said a woman in the automatic laundry. 'But I ask you outsiders, just what would we do then?' "

"NEW YORK—The stock market tiptoed gingerly into 1971 after having vigorously danced out of 1970."

It's agreed that every lead can't be a masterpiece, but they all should be written in a simple, uncomplicated manner that doesn't confuse—and lose—the reader.

"DUESSELDORF—Sources close to the West German Iron and Steel Federation said today they discount President Nixon's threat to invite more steel imports from Western European and Japanese producers, following a rise in prices by Bethlehem Steel Co." How about using two sentences?

Under "What Did He Say?" we have this not so good lead:

"WASHINGTON—The Post Office has directed postmasters to stop holding up payments to pornography dealers abroad, a top official said today." Are the postmasters paying pornography dealers?

OMISSION of that often causes ambiguity. An example in the report:

"NEW YORK—Drivers and spokesmen for the taxi industry said Wednesday business has fallen off since the 15-day cab strike last month." Wonder why only Wednesday business has fallen off?

"EXPLAIN, Explain"

Under this heading the report comments:

"Getting the reader past the lead and into the body of the story is not enough. After we get him there we must answer all of his questions, at least all of the important ones.

"When you answer his questions, you've got a satisfied customer."

For instance:

". . . When writing about the Hyden mine disaster, Sy Ramsey didn't leave his readers wondering what primer cord is and why its use is restricted. He told 'em: 'Primer cord, a ropelike explosives detonator, is forbidden in underground mines because it flashes and flames.' "

In reverse:

A Jan. 22 story said Sen. Ellender was elected president pro tem of the Senate, but it didn't say what the president pro tem is or does. (We know, but do all our readers know?) The explanation was given in a Jan. 25 story when Ellender first presided over the Senate.

THE AP committee got literary and quoted Shakespeare's "As You Like It," Act I, Scene 2:

CELIA: . . . Here comes Monsieur LeBeau.

ROSALIND: With his mouth full of news.

CELIA: Which he will put on us as pigeons feed their young.

ROSALIND: Then we will be news-crammed.

Observed the report: News Crammed. Yes, that's what the AP report should be. And our newspapers. But *not* all in lead sentences! Consider:

"WASHINGTON (Feb. 18)—President Nixon proposed today a six-point, low-budgeted package of proposals to insure adequate medical care for all American families through a vast expansion of private insurance and reorganization of the medical care system.

"In a 17-page message to Congress, Nixon offered a comprehensive alternative to Democratic proposals for national health insurance by emphasizing federally stimulated reforms of the current medical care program."

Said an AP committee critic: "Leaving aside the fact that the first sentence diagrams as Nixon/Proposed/Package/of/Proposals . . . listen to this comment from a reader:

" 'I don't really need to know in the lead that it's a six-point, low-budgeted package. Couldn't it just have said the President had proposed that every American family be insured for medical care?'

"I suspect the trouble was that the reporter knew more than his readers. He knew the Democrats had proposed full national medical insurance, that Nixon was taking a different tack. And so he stressed low-budgeted and comprehensive alternative. I submit, however, that 'six-point,' '17-page' and such lint-collecting items slow up the story."

But balancing the bad with some "nice things" (fragging again) were these leads:

HOUSTON (Feb. 5) by Howard Benedict—"Two Americans . . . walked the dusty surface of the moon today, ghostly figures seeking the secrets of an alien land."

LAS VEGAS, NEV. (Feb. 13) by Terry Ryan—"A red light may soon shine amidst the neon of Las Vegas." (The DA has drafted an ordinance to legalize prostitution.)

Carl C. Craft, (Feb. 17)—"A little guy from Rocky Hill, Conn., came to Capital Hill Wednesday to ask when Washington is going to stop talking and start doing something about pollution. It's ruining his fishing hole." (A fine one-two punch!)

If this isn't enough, we find that there are difficulties in covering the arts.

Reporting on music, painting and sculpture presents some problems similar to those encountered in writing about scientific developments and the approach to handling them ought to be the same. Technical matter should be described in lucid terms without biting off more than one can chew.

The AP's obituary of Igor Stravinsky (New York, April 6) is an example of sound research and smooth writing with a few elegant technical terms tossed in. But a closer look reveals some errors (Stravinsky's close associate, Robert Craft, wrote books *with* Stravinsky and not *about* him) and some terminology that is meaningless to either the expert or the uninformed.

There is no value to the lay reader, the report said, in using such terms as "polytonal," "the 12-tone system" and "atonality."

And, it seems it is difficult to keep away from emerging vogue words. They are also called words-to-watch-out-for-before-they-become-entrenched-in-the-language. Such as

Disincentives

Quantifying

One to One

Low profiles.

The committee liked this piece of sports writing:

"NEW YORK—It's several hours before the big game and here are the big, burly football players about to partake of some nice, thick . . . pancakes.

"Pancakes?

"You bet your Aunt Jemima and don't spare the syrup, says Dr. Donald L. Cooper, team physician at Oklahoma State University. Steak, the doctor says, is a no-no. . . .""

Just in case you missed it, another piece is worth repeating. It is Mark Brown's profile of J. Edgar Hoover, which began:

"Had circumstances been different 60 years ago, John Edgar Hoover might have been a man of God. And what a hell-fire and brimstone preacher he would have been.

"Instead, the young Hoover turned his passion to a more secular calling—to uphold the laws of man. And what a hell-fire and brimstone cop he has been."

Writers frequently miss the right word, the committee members found. The word *claim* is often used instead of *says; following* in place of *after.*

Tornadoes are still *spawned.* What do they do? They *rake.* They *swoop* and they *spew destruction.*

AN APPROPRIATE word at the end of the last report:

"To sum up, here is a character named Mr. Bolter in "Oliver Twist":

"What's the good of talking in that way to me; why don't yer speak so as I can understand yer?"

Why can't writers say what they mean? Why do they have to camouflage their work with a barrage of verbiage that buries the poor reader? James L. Julian, professor emeritus of journalism at San Diego State University, explores the word gimmicks so prevalent in journalism, in a March 1978 essay.

WORD GIMMICKS

James L. Julian

Is camouflaged communication becoming a way of life? Do we really need it to make life more bearable?

Take some ads from a newspaper. Mobile home "estates" are available in spacious 12' by 24' plots. Then there's a "kinderkollege" for ages 2 to 5—just the ego trip for doting parents. And there's beer in full half-quart cans.

The unutterable becomes utterable by euphemistic gimmicks. A fellow places a want ad for a woman with whom to have "a meaningful relationship" (sex exclusively with him), another wants to meet a "modern (easily bedded) girl," and a third seeks "female companionship for daylight meetings" (he can't sneak out nights on his wife).

An ad offering "previously owned cars" is topped by one listing "experienced furniture" for sale. "Good transportation car" usually translates as, "It's a clunker."

Unsavory ideas inevitably get sugared with new terminology. The head of a local welfare agency wants that title changed to Income Security Department. The state unemployment office became the Human Resources Agency. After their whopping pay raises, congressmen would no longer take those long, frequent recesses. House members would toil in district work periods. And the Senate would schedule non-legislative periods to go home or junketing.

The city is adding an animal control officer (dog catcher) and is selling some mobile response units (cops' prowl cars). A university has an opening at the entry-level salary (the pay is poor) for typists in its Word Processing Center (steno pool). Companies aver to have affirmative action programs (white males needn't apply).

A fellow said on telly that there would be "an indigenation of all natural resources after democratic rule is established in Rhodesia." He meant that white-owned farms and mines would be up for grabs after the coming takeover.

There's a bit of drollery in a matronly woman of generous physical proportions referring to "a visit to the little girls' room."

California teems with illegal aliens. After complaints by Mexican-America groups about such demeaning labels, the media now call them undocumented aliens.

As an old geezer, now dubbed a golden-ager and senior citizen (How come my kids aren't dross-agers or junior citizens?), I recollect when today's adult entertainment vehicles were called dirty movies. We had jails and prisons in lieu of rehabilitation centers and correctional facilities.

In school, we knew who the smart kids were and who the dumb ones were, and we said so. Now they're tagged as eager learners, gifted, exceptional, under-achievers, and mentally disadvantaged with learning disabilities or cultural deprivations. The baddies were whisked to detention hall or paddled. Now they're assigned to the Human Ecology Detail for behavior modification.

One classmate had, in today's language, a character disorder with antisocial inclinations and manifestations of hostility in his interpersonal relationships. We just called him a big bully. We weren't surprised later when one of his victims employed a firearm to accomplish termination of his vital functions.

Examples of verbal mincy-toeing are plentiful in any path we tread. Governments make preemptive strikes (sneak attacks) or launch protective reaction missions (hit 'em before they're ready) or consummate a police action against an aggressor (undeclared war), deal with developing or emerging (primitive, backward) nations, implement terminatable disciplinary action against employees (fire them) to eschew impairing the mission capability of their personnel (avoid flubbing the job).

TV warns "due to the nature of tonight's program, parental discretion is advised" (the show's loaded with vulgarity, raw violence juicy sex) and credits "promotional consideration furnished by Risky Airlines" (we mooched travel costs as a swap for this plugola).

Social planners worry about economically disadvantaged citizens (poor folks) and youthful offenders (teenage hoodlums) living in the inner city (muggers' and rapists' special hunting preserve). In an effort to achieve social justice (spread around other people's loot), they clash with politicians lacking sensitivity (not the bleeding-heart types), who are unresponsive to people's needs (unwilling to raise taxes). This can impose hardships on energetically deprived persons (lazy bums).

Public inspection officers (vice squads) often bust sellers of magazines and films designed for mature audiences (fans of prurient voyeuristic titillations).

Cheers for legislators who act in the pubic interest (anything benefiting me), close tax loopholes (exemptions you get, but I don't), provide economically sound tax incentives (loopholes for me), and enact long-needed tax reforms (cut my taxes, raise yours).

Rhetorical overkill can be transparent. If I complain that many euphemisms are male bovine excreted organic matter, you can see my words as pure bullstuff.

If readers often think they've read something before, Jack Botts, a journalism professor at the University of Nebraska, says it's no accident. In a March 1972 essay, he discusses what he calls the "tired, tired words" that writers seem to overuse while they allow others to rust for lack of use.

THOSE TIRED, TIRED WORDS

Jack Botts

HOW MANY TIMES have you read a newspaper story with the vague, unsatisfied feeling that you had passed that way before? Something about the story seemed familiar, even though the information was new.

All new but the words. Few words are really new, of course. Some may seem new because they are used rarely. Others, because they are overused or abused, steal meaning and dissolve stories in irritating grayness.

Few of us take the time to examine closely how we and our fellow journalists use words, the tools of our profession. If we did, it may shock us to learn that nearly everyone is careless and lazy with those tools.

We may find that although some words are rusted from lack of use, many other words and phrases have worn badly. Some of them may have been good tools at one time, but they no longer cut cleanly and accurately.

If you are interested in the condition of journalism's tool chest, check your local newspaper or, better yet, the news wire service. Either of the basic wire services reflect general news writing quality.

I made some discoveries recently when reading the entire report of a basic news wire for one week. It had been more than five years since I had done that. It used to be my job (for about 16 years) to read several wires. This time I read copy as a member of a wire service writing study committee.

I discovered that the language of news changes more rapidly than I had realized when I was wire editor for a daily newspaper. I was expecting to find the same worn and misshapen language tools that I had noticed years before.

They weren't there. I found no instance of a U.S. senator "lashing out" at the Administration. Nobody "flayed" his critics in 1972, apparently. But as I crossed off the tired words and phrases of 5 or 10 years ago, I found new ones to add to my list. An entirely new set of worn-out word tools had supplanted those I expected to find.

Most of us simply, and gradually, substitute one set of worn out tools for another. By the time we recognize the wear and discard one, we have allowed another to take its place.

Story-weary phrases are unimpressive. They hang alone like bones, unadorned with the meat and juices of a story.

Following is a little nonsense tale to catalog today's inventory of writing tools that need discarding, and to remind us that as professionals we owe our language greater respect:

UPPER HOMBERG, SASK (xxxx)—CHANCELLOR HELMUT VON FENSZITTER CALLED TUESDAY FOR A TOP-LEVEL GATHERING OF A MAJORITY OF HIS NATION'S LEADERS TO MAKE A FAR-REACHING INQUIRY INTO A HOST OF PROBLEMS THAT HAVE APPEARED IN THE WAKE OF STEPPED-UP CRITICISM AT HOME.

HE RULED OUT A MARATHON SESSION IN ANTICIPATION THAT HE MIGHT COME UNDER ATTACK FROM HIS OPPONENTS.

HIS ACTION WAS PRECIPITATED BY SWEEPING GAINS IN UNEMPLOYMENT WHICH HE SAYS HAVE PLACED JOBLESS FIGURES OVER THE MARK OF A YEAR AGO.

THE CHANCELLOR ANNOUNCED THAT HIS EFFORTS WERE INTENSIFIED TO SERVE NOTICE THAT HIS ADMINISTRATION EXPRESS OPTIMISM AMID REPORTS THAT HIS BUDGET FALLS SHORT OF BEING A POWERFUL DETERRENT TO INFLATION.

HE SAID HE IS TAKING PRELIMINARY STEPS WITH A MINIMUM OF DELAY TO STEM THE RISING TIDE OF APATHY. A FOCAL POINT OF HIS PROGRAM IS DESIGNED TO PRODUCE THE ADDED BONUS OF CLOSED RANKS AT HOME AND GROWING TIES ABROAD.

HE SAID HIS ADVISERS ARE WEIGHING A SUGGESTION TO RELEASE PREVIOUSLY UNDISCLOSED DETAILS WHICH ARE BEING MAPPED BY HIS STAFF. THEY WILL PRESS FOR APPROVAL, BUT THE CHANCELLOR SHIED AWAY FROM DISCUSSING POLLS WHICH INDICATE THAT THE MAJOR OBSTACLE MAY SURFACE NEXT WEEK.

LAST WEEK'S MARGIN OF VICTORY CLIMAXED AN EFFORT OF TWO-MONTHS DURATION BY THE STAFF. IT STRUCK DOWN A LEADERSHIP MOVE WHICH MUSTERED ONLY EIGHT VOTES AND CLOSELY PARALLELED A SIMILAR ACTION TRIGGERED A YEAR AGO.

IN THE AFTERMATH OF THAT SKIRMISH, ADMINISTRATIVE LIEUTENANTS BRUSHED ASIDE CRITICS WHO WERE QUOTED AS SAYING THAT A MAJOR SHARE OF THE BLAME STEMS FROM OVEROPTIMISM.

TAKING A FIRM STAND AGAINST MALCONTENTS, THE CHAN-
CELLOR SPELLED OUT HIS CONVICTIONS BUT STOPPED SHORT OF
NAME-CALLING IN LINE WITH NEW POLICIES AIMED AT CREATING
A BETTER IMAGE. HE EXPRESSED CONCERN ABOUT HIS SPEECH,
WHICH WAS MARKED BY APPLAUSE, AND IN WHICH HE EMPLOYED
SHORTER WORDS IN AN EFFORT TO STAY WITHIN THE TIME
LIMIT.

IN RESPONSE TO SUGGESTIONS BY LETTER WRITERS, HIS
COMMENTS WERE BELIEVED TO BE HIGHLIGHTED BY LONGER
PAUSES, WHICH MAY BE HAILED AS SWEEPING SUCCESSES.

Sometimes, the wrong word in the wrong place can change the meaning of a sentence, indeed, a story. It can convey opinion and cast doubt on the objectivity of the entire piece. In this February 1972 essay, Lee J. Dudek of the University of South Carolina, examines the damage that can be done with *only.*

ONLY IN REPORTING

Lee J. Dudek

OF THE 111,080 returns filed by Feb. 19, 1970, 7,107 . . . had errors. Of the 113,217 this year, *only* 4,189 had errors." (Columbia *State,* April 14, 1971)

"Labor Secretary James Hodgson calls the increase in consumer prices of *only* two tenths of one per cent last month 'Good News.' " (UPI wire, March 19, 1971)

"There were 142 strikes of local-government employees in 1966 . . . vs. *only* 42 the year before." (*Newsweek,* June 28, 1971, p. 78)

Question: What *news value* does that "only" in each of the above quotes serve?

General semanticists and psychologists subscribe to a proposition to the effect, "When Peter talks about Paul we learn more about Peter than we do about Paul." Take the use of "only" in news stories.

In the first item, the number of tax form errors dropped from 6.4 per cent to about 3.6 per cent. The reporter obviously never worked in an internal revenue office. Were he to translate those *only* 4,189 erroneous forms into the number of man hours required to correct them and the cost to taxpayers, would he still have used the qualifier?

Labor Secretary Hodgson might find a .2 per cent consumer price index rise "good news." So might the writer of our second item. But at a time of record high unemployment and a continuously shrinking dollar, is *any* further decline in buying power a matter of "only"?

Apparently the *Newsweek* writer of item three was not affected by the stench, litter, dangers, travel and other inconveniences of a government employees strike in 1965 since he finds 42 such interruptions of vital services negligible enough to describe with an "only."

United Press International on Dec. 16, 1971, said this when former Illinois Gov. Otto Kerner made news as a federal appeals court judge: "Kerner, 63, is *only* the fourth federal judge in history to be indicted by a federal grand

jury." So why the fuss? The charges were *only* bribery, mail fraud, tax eva-
sion, perjury, and conspiracy. This UPI writer's use of "only" here reminds
me of the college newspaper story of Nov. 4, 1963 that read, "John Kennedy
is only the fourth American President to be assassinated."

Or take for example:

Item: "Three operators of the anti-war U-F-O Coffeehouse in Columbia
have had their jail sentences reduced from six years to *only* two years, suspended on a one-year probation." (UPI wire, April 16, 1971) Later, UPI
changed that "only" to a "simply."

What are the reporting qualifications of anyone who refers to a two-year
prison stretch as though it were "only" and "simply" in a prison hardly no-
torious for its comforts?

The next two items may provide some explanation for that "only" in the
.2 per cent price rise story as perhaps denoting both a minute number and a
relatively negligible quantity. What can be the value of a dollar now when a
UPI writer can quote (without quotation marks) a Pentagon spokesman: "The
Defense Department is spending $30.4 *million* in this fiscal year for over-all
public information activities and plans to spend *only* $24.9 *million* for fiscal
1972, starting July 1."? (UPI, Washington, March 7, 1971)

Or try this one:

"The SEC will accept rates that will increase Wall Street incomes by
$400 *million*. The $15 (present) charge brings in *only* $300 *million*." (*News-
week*, May 10, 1971, p. 23)

Unfortunately, we get no guidance here from the recorder of "Winners
and Sinners" in the New York *Times*. Theodore M. Bernstein refers to "only"
in his "Watch Your Language" as to "proper positioning" in a sentence—
only.

The Oxford Dictionary (1961 edition, vol. 11, p. 127) provides one clue.
"Only" implies that the number following it is apparently inconsequential as
viewed from the perspective of the writer of his news medium.

Original spellings of the little four-lettered beast include "onely, onelye,
onelie." In Old English it meant unique, solitary, singular, excellent. The third
Oxford definition listed is "one, no more." As an adjective, "only" currently
"limits the statement to a single or defined person, thing or number . . . one,
solely, merely, exclusively." Hence, there are more objections to "only."

The use of "only" in reporting tends to be either a labelling of the obvious or an overt/covert editorial slanting. The basic fault in thoughtless uses
of "only" seems to be the covering of a significant reality behind a compar-
atively insignificant quantity.

Or, it could be a reflection of an apparent growing insensitivity to values—property, monetary, human suffering and even life.

Overstatement? Then cogitate this gem. "The Zodiac has boasted of killing 13 persons, but police have postively linked the killer to *only* five murders." (UPI, Napa, Calif., March 7, 1971) At what number of slayings does that writer place the right to "boast of killing"?

Or take this final example which deserves some sort of prize as a commentary on journalism and our times. "Last Labor Day weekend . . . up to 725 auto deaths were predicted—but *only* 612 *persons actually died."* (*Newsweek,* Sept. 7, 1970, p. 54) To a letter objecting to that use of "only" (Nov. 24, 1970), the reply was made, "We do not really feel that our use of the term was callous." Why not? Because, "In situations where many deaths were expected but *few* occurred, it is often more important to inform the reader that things might have been worse than to imply that whatever happened was an unmitigated disaster."

If 612 deaths are *few,* if 612 deaths are *not* an unmitigated disaster, what does *Newsweek* call *many* and an *actual* unmitigated disaster?

The women's movement has had a number of effects on American life since the movement began in the late 1960s. Equality has been achieved in many areas; the fight for it goes on in others. The arguments over the style to use in describing the movement and women in general, however, have been almost as fierce as the battles in the legislative chambers and company boardrooms.

A series of essays in *The Quill* considers the problem.

*First, in July 1974, Zena Beth McGlashan, now at the University of North Dakota, discusses the early reluctance of stylebook compilers and copy editors to avoid identifying a woman as being married.

*In the July-August 1977 issue, Donald M. Williams, who teaches journalism at Baylor University, decries the end to making distinctions in print between men and women.

*In October 1980, Jean Ward of the University of Minnesota journalism faculty, goes beyond titles to get at the sexist presumptions and attitudes she still finds prevalent in journalism.

*In January 1981, R. Thomas Berner, an assistant professor of journalism at Pennsylvania State University and the author of *Language Skills for Journalists and Editing,* continues the discussion by talking about the tendency to "neuter" all copy. At the time this anthology was compiled, he was completing work on his third book, *Literary Journalism.*

'MS.,' 'MISS,' 'MRS.' AS ANTIQUATED AS 'MR.'

Zena Beth McGlashan

2.20 *Do not abbreviate Alexander, Benjamin, Charles, Frederick, William, etc., as Alec, Alex, Ben., Benj., Chas., etc. unless person does so himself. Follow person's preference.*

— *United Press International Newswire Stylebook*

WILLIAM BUCKLEY could be Wm. if his conservative nature would allow him such a zippy appellation. President Truman was Harry S with no period—that's the way it was—period.

But good luck if Mrs. Arnold L. Wattenmiller, chairperson of the Civic Improvement Committee's sub-committee on parks, wants to be Irene Wattenmiller. Her hometown newspaper will most likely insist that she be Mrs. Arnold L., not Irene.

As far as most of the nation's print media are concerned, Arnold is a "person," but Irene isn't. He has "preference," but she doesn't.

Back in my first years of being a women's editor, I argued with women who insisted on their "own" names. Ideas about women's identity came slowly to me, because I was first a journalist—and then a woman. And style was style.

"A woman takes her husband's name when she marries and keeps it until she is widowed or unless she is divorced." I would patiently explain to those women who kept insisting about a then-vague term, "identity."

Journalists—whose job it is to chronicle change—seem slowest to alter their thinking—or their sacred style. A woman should be allowed her own identity—that idea has slowly overtaken me, a woman journalist, and it is making snail-like entrance into print.

When the Ms. mess began in earnest, thanks to Gloria Steinem, Pat Carbine, and all those inspired women who've stirred the magazine world with a slick-paper revolution, a friend of mine who works on the copy desk of the Los Angeles *Times* voiced an objection to its use:

"How will we be able to tell if a woman is married or not?"

"What difference does it make?," I asked, not without hostility. "What do you want—three categories? Married women, Mrs.; never-married, Miss, and then hand out the Ms. title to the divorcees?"

My final shot was: "How do you tell if a man is married or not?"

His puzzled look indicated that he'd not thought of it quite that way before.

The blanket designation Ms. is not the answer, either. Consider this from a press release sent out by Los Angeles Mayor Tom Bradley's office about a committee on the status of women: "Chairpersons are Ms. Hallie Tenner and Ms. Opal Jones."

Ms. is the flag waved by the mayor's press people to say, hey, we got the message—we know all about that women's movement stuff. Why can't they just be Hallie Tenner and Opal Jones?

If a person clears away the cynicism or the simple confusion and looks at the style guide with less than a traditional eye, the answer could be simple. Personal preference on first reference, last name after that.

Let Jane Smith be Smith on second reference. And if she heads the Say No on Off-Shore Drilling Association and her husband, Warren, just happens to be on the board of Standard Oil, then the reporter will surely add, "Smith's husband, Warren, is on the board of. . . ."

However, if Warren runs a coin shop and couldn't care less about oil or the shoreline, then he deserves no mention.

During a vacation stint on the Santa Monica *Evening Outlook,* I was obliged to type great lists of names under the common heading Mmes.—plural of Madame—some affectation of a long-deceased society editor which has been a cross-like burden for the nation's women's departments ever since. "On the committee are Mmes. John Jones, Harold Armour, Xavier L. Bascome, Seymour D. Arnst . . ." and so on.

No one can know what a curse this is until the assignment, either women's page or city-side, is given: "Find out if this Maybelle Arnst is Mrs. Seymour D. Arnst."

Why? Maybe Maybelle listed her name that way because she wants to be Maybelle. Maybe her membership on the committee is because she likes the work being done, not because she wants to boost Seymour's social, business and economic standing.

If a woman can use either the Mrs. designation or a first name-last name basis, shouldn't a man be allowed to equal treatment? Sure. Mr. Harold Jones can be Mr. if he insists. But chances are he won't.

He's heard it from his Little League coach, his high school gym teacher, bellowed by a drill sergeant—all his life, that last name designation has been used, both in good humor and bad. Harold Jones, unless he teaches school, probably doesn't think of himself as Mr. Jones.

That same conditioning process can work for women, too. At first it will look a bit odd for Ann Jones to be second-referenced as Jones. But it will look no more strange than the style used by the New York *Times*—which clings to "Mr."

Newspapers, and their readers, could most easily adapt to the new style if it were used gradually.

The 23-year-old career woman most likely would not object to the last-name style. However, if the story concerns Emma Jones who is 90 and refers to traveling on the Greyhound bus as "taking the stage," second reference would be to Mrs. Jones.

Let the title fit the person. The late Rep. Jeanette Rankin of Montana would have been delighted to be second-referenced as Rankin. That was her style.

THE CASE AGAINST 'KATZMAURER'S BRA'

Donald M. Williams

Some of the easier victories of The Women's Movement have been scored against the American press. Mighty editors, having received a few stiff letters on organizational stationery from chairpersons and an impassioned note

This article appeared in the magazine under the title, "Don't Call Her Ms. It was All A Mstake."

or two on copy paper from their own cub newspersons, have quickly, too quickly, agreed to quit making the old distinctions between men and women in their papers.

This, I submit, is suppression and bad journalism. Both as a traditionalist and as a university teacher, I protest. Of course, I protest also as a man; but I might just as reasonably do so if I were a woman. I am afraid that the yielding editors, though perhaps intending only a bow to The Movement, are going to change the world, and in ways that the world will not welcome.

A livable world must recognize that men and women are different from each other and that *equal* does not mean *identical*. Distinctions based on sex are, I think, in accord with nature. But they have persisted because the world has chosen to preserve them. If the world is led to cast them aside as outmoded, their naturalness will not save them. And consider: to lead the world in innovations, good and bad, who has more influence than the United States? To lead the United States in the same ways, who more than the press?

Probably in an attempt to be nation-leaders, some newspapers have begun dropping the titles before women's surnames. Once they have identified a woman in a news or feature story as Elizabeth Jones or Mrs. John Jones, they call her subsequently only "Jones." The fancy is that this treatment bestows equality upon women; their names are just like men's names now. Obviously, this gesture pleases The Movement. That does not mean it pleases all women or most women. My wife is at the very least my equal, but she is not my double; she is not "Williams." She would be angry at any reporter who took it for granted that she wanted to be, and her feeling is not unique among women.

This aberration is, besides, confusing to the reader. In references to one of two people, good sense tells us to indicate which one we have in mind. If the two are husband and wife, then "Jones" will not serve for now this one, now that one. If several people of both sexes are being considered, it is only intelligent to distinguish the sex when the discussion narrows—and our way of distinguishing is to give titles to the women, though not necessarily to the men. Failing this help, a reader can hardly, among John Jones, Patsy Kent, Mabel Green, Roger Smith, Deborah Katzmaurer and Kevin Marmorfeder, remember which one is meant by, say, "Kent." The reader backtracks until he finds the full name: "Oh, yes; this one is a woman." Some may reply, "Well, it doesn't matter." But to most newspaper readers, I suggest, it does matter; it has always mattered. Female is not male. Besides, vague identification is bad journalism. Why not use a convenient "Mrs." or "Miss" for the women, call the men "Jones," "Smith," and "Marmorfeder," and be clear?

Of course, the press as a whole is not yet violating sense and tradition in this manner. The AP-UPI stylebook has helped; and the long-due revision also discountenances last-naming women, except on the sports wire. The New York Times, with its own famous stylebook, is sticking with "Miss" and "Mrs."

except in a few specified circumstances. In South Dakota, where I sojourned lately, only 12 of the 114 newspapers that replied to a recent questionnaire said they customarily use the last-name-only style for women, and all of those are weeklies. (Sports stories have been an exception for a good many papers and will become so for more after the new wire service book comes out. Perhaps it is not so offensive to have the discus thrower or the miler, in a story about a girls' track meet, called "Jones." On the other hand, why assume that female athletes are less feminine than other women?)

Last-naming, though not in general use, is not isolated, either. According to an informal survey made last year, some large papers have yielded— the Pittsburgh Post-Gazette, the Oakland Tribune, the Miami News, the Houston Post, the Des Moines Register and Tribune, the Washington Post. The Gannett organization has gone along. And there are others. Nearly all campus papers, furthermore, refer to great-grandmothers and college girls alike as "Jones." College reporters have a way of graduating and getting jobs on newspapers; and if they carry their youthful convictions and lesser impulses into their professional lives, the number of papers of general circulation reporting that "Green and Karzmaurer poured tea" seems likely to increase.

Along with the as yet rather few papers that be-Jones and be-Katzmaurer women, there are many indeed that on occasion be-Ms. them. This practive is authorized by the AP-UPI stylebook, though only at the woman's request—hence the felicitous phrase, "Ms. Higgins, who prefers that title, said. . . ." But not many papers use "Ms." indiscriminately to include both the divorced Boston lawyer and the Iowa farm wife, up to her ears in jars and kettles as she cans corn and green beans for next year's harvest hands. (In the South Dakota poll, none did this.)

Some papers seem to let each reporter refer to women as he likes; in the same paper, under different bylines, women are "Miss" or "Mrs.," or "Ms.," and "Jones." In these cases, I smell retreat, for editors do not otherwise let reporters decide matters of style. Whether to call pastors "the Rev. Mr. Jones" or simply "Jones," whether to write "twelve" or "12," whether to abbreviate "street" and "avenue"—these questions are decided by the paper and its stylebook, not by reportorial whim or bias.

This sort of thing reflects editorial indecisiveness rather than policy. But much of the press has in fact adopted, at least tacitly, some policies that were inspired by the muses of Ms. In particular, many newspapers now refrain from publishing the standard rainy-day photograph of the pretty-girl-having-trouble-with-her-umbrella (and, incidentally, -skirt). I know too many news editors too well to imagine that the profession has suddenly and unaccountably turned beauty-blind.

And a good many newspaper editorial staffs have no doubt had visited upon them, by their editors and editresses, directives like the one that recently went around the newsroom of one large Eastern paper. The missive advises reporters to avoid snickers at the Women's Movement, to omit irrelevant mention of a woman's attire or her figure, and by other measures of omission or commission to eliminate any presumption that the newspaper is a man. Some of the measures are reasonable and fair, but the closing instruction makes up for them. "As a final test," the reporters are told, "try the turnabout approach when writing about a woman. Would you say the same thing about a man?" This, I submit, is a test of identical treatment—"the same thing"—and not of equal treatment.

I have been enumerating some mainly verbal practices, and I know very well that in these days when self-expression is everything, words are supposed to be nothing. Of course, I disagree. Words are enough to darken in us the habit of distinguishing between manhood and womanhood and to make us shrug at marriage and its meaning. If to do these things is indeed the plan, I think the chances of realization are strong. Newspapers, radio and television may be powerful enough tdoay to destroy an idea, as in George Orwell's "1984," by suppressing the words that convey it. Sexual indiscriminateness is turning our language to murk and our spirits to custard.

To uphold the value of the traditional distinctions is not to advocate unfairness. Kindness and clearsighted appreciation of ability and worth have no enemy in tradition. So, the thesis that men and women are different—not unequal, but different—is respectable to voice and to act upon.

The same impulses that led some editors to refer to women as if they were men are also behind the determination, in certain quarters, not to have women "treated as sex objects." No normal man considers womanhood as merely physical. The Movement, though, not recognizing pretty distinctions, erases "merely" and begrudges men (and women) the pleasure of mentioning this attribute of women anywhere.

By the same reasoning that translates *equal as identical,* men must not be thrilled or moved at the sight of a lovely woman. The Lord knows, I still cherish my right to express joy in the sight of a pretty knee or waistline or bosom or eye. I feel as entitled to my pleasure as if it were somehow—well, natural. And though the pretext for the newspapers' girl-and-umbrella pictures was usually weak and the accompanying prose silly—give them back anyway, O Editors. I, for one, will promise to try to remember: the girl is indubitably a human being in the general sense as well as a female in the particular, unquestionably the possessor of attributes other than those salient in this photograph, indisputably not a mere sex object. (Fie upon those who think of her as mere.)

Newspapers bereave half their readers of a small delight by middle-drawering such pictures for the enjoyment of only their own male copyreaders and news editors; but the papers that yield on the question of women's titles do much more: they withhold information from their readers. The premise is that readers should not desire to know whether a person is male or female, whether a woman is married or single. But whether they should or should not so desire, many or most of them, I maintain, do. These things have always made a difference. Why should a minority of zealots be able so easily to persuade even a few editors that the caprice of this instant is more valid than the wisdom of always? In what way is it a valid assumption that all women want to conceal their marital status or, practically, their sex?

If we say that sex does not matter and that a woman's marital status does not matter, then we have to say that the countless and immemorial deeds of sacrifice and heroism performed by women acting specifically as women and as wives and mothers do not matter. And till now, these deeds have been implanted in out attitudes and implicit in our standards. If a woman's marital status does not matter, then marriage does not matter. If marriage does not matter, farewell, family. And farewell, civilization.

Editors may think that in substituting new words for traditional ones they are only being indulgent and that their decision goes no further than the printed page. Of all people, editors ought to know better: words are always springing off pages and slipping away in search of crowds.

THE WAR OF WORDS

Jean Ward

A funny thing happened on the way to equality in news coverage. Through the early 1970s, newsrooms all over were rife with arguments about "ms." and "chairperson" and the masculine pronouns. By 1977, the revised Associated Press Stylebook, as well as countless style manuals for other news organizations, was out with pronouncements on style and remedies for sexism.

The AP sounds stern on equal treatement in its section on "women" (p. 240).

> *Women should receive the same treatment as men in all areas of coverage. Physical descriptions, sexist references, demeaning stereotypes and condescending phrases should not be used.*
> *—Copy should not assume maleness when both sexes are involved, as in* Jackson told newsmen *or in* the taxpayer . . . he *when it easily can* be said *Jackson told reporters or taxpayers . . . they.*
> *—Copy should not express surprise that* an attractive woman can be professionally accomplished, *as in:* Mary Smith doesn't look the part but she's an authority on . . .

—Copy should not gratuitously mention family relationships when there is no relevance to the subject, as in: *Golda Meir, a doughty grandmother, told the Egyptians today . . .*

—Use the same standards for men and women in deciding whether to include specific mention of personal appearance or marital and family situation.

In other words, treatment of the sexes should be even-handed and free of assumptions and stereotypes. This does not mean that valid and acceptable words such as mankind or humanity cannot be used. They are proper.

But sexism in the news hasn't gone away. Titles and pronouns are among the easy parts of the new stylebooks; it is relatively simple to detect lapses in these areas. But more deeply rooted sexist presumptions and attitudes have a way of emerging from journalistic writing and slipping past editors, well-intentioned though they may be.

For instance, it's easier to order that "copy should not assume maleness" than to make the rule stick, as the following journalistic examples show:

Most alcoholics are either employed persons or working housewives, he said.

Legal history was made when a man was granted a high court order restraining a woman neighbor from enticing away his dog.

While the examples above make it clear that maleness is assumed, consider the complications when a racial component is added:

A federal judge ordered New York state's virtually all-male, all-white police, force to give half of its job openings for years to come to women and members of minority groups. U.S. District Judge James Foley said a quota system of 40 percent blacks and Hispanics and 10 percent women would have to be followed until the overall 3,400-member force approximately reflects the racial makeup of the population it serves—a process that apparently would take at least five years.

How's that again? Are the judge and the journalists assuming that the 40 percent quota of blacks-Hispanics is male *and* female and that the 10 percent women are white women? Or that the 40 percent quota will be male minorities and the 10 percent quota will be females of all races? Or what?

Even if a publication's staff members stop writing stories that reveal a sexist voice on the part of the reporter, remaining problems plague the writer who quotes sexist sources. A computer programmer was quoted in the New York *Times* as saying, "There's no real commonality among programmers. I don't know that we beat our wives any more than anyone else." A professor of economics, Barbara Bergman, objected:

"That remark didn't deserve a place in a factual article for two reasons—its smug and revolting sexism and its wishful concealment of the fact that a lot of programmers don't have wives—they have husbands."

Similarly, the New York *Times'* editors allowed a guest column by Walt Frazier to assert:

> For too many black kids, their idols aren't even athletes. Their idols are pimps—the guys they see with the big cars, the flashy clothes and women.

A careful sports editor would have reminded the Knickerbockers team member that at least half of the black kids are female.

And in Minneapolis, a member of the Star's board of contributors undertook an article criticizing the Star's local coverage with this lead:

> On May 9, five blacks broke into the Minneapolis home of a white schoolteacher, beat him, raped his wife, and smashed and looted everything they could find. If you're a reader of this newspaper, you didn't see a word of the incident until Tuesday, May 15, six days later. Why?

Evidently the editors were so preoccupied with his criticism of the coverage that they failed to suggest a rewrite: On May 9, five blacks broke into the home of a Minneapolis couple, beat the man (or husband) and raped the woman (or wife). Or did they notice and let the revealingly sexist sentence run, and allow their critic to be vulnerable to attack for his sexism?

A related problem involves copy from such organizations as the Gallup Poll. Many of the questions in earlier decades have been repeated over time to show opinion shift on a topic. Thus, this poll and others continue to use questions with outmoded terms and questions that reveal a sex-role stereotype of earlier decades. For instance, in 1945 and subsequently, respondents were asked, "If you had a son, would you like to see him go into politics as a life's work?" And as late as 1974, Gallup offered a new question that ignored females when it asked: "Would you favor or oppose requiring all young men to give one year of service in the nation—either in the military forces or in nonmilitary work here or abroad, such as VISTA or the Peace Corps?"

The habit of ignoring women in public life may help to account for an astounding lapse into "all people are male" thinking that seems to have escaped editors, at Gallup and elsewhere, who in late August 1978 published this report:

> Blacks have made considerable headway in American society since the "March on Washington" 15 years ago, and a record number of people today say they would vote for a black for president and would not object to blacks as neighbors. . . . Prejudice toward a black presidential candidate has declined to the lowest point yet recorded.

The big problem with their conclusion is that Gallup didn't ask about willingness to vote for a black but rather asked about willingness to vote for

a "Negro man," as the question printed right in the report for everyone—
including editors—to see reveals:

> There's always much discussion about the qualifications of presi-
> dential candidates—their education, age, race, religion and the like. If
> your party nominated a generally well-qualified man for president and he
> happened to be a Negro would you vote for him?

Not only did the poll ignore women as potential candidates, it went on
to generalize from a question about a "Negro man" to the entire black population.

In sum, editors receive copy from a variety of sources who evidently think
either that all people are men or unwittingly imply that women are not people.
Certainly there are difficult questions to be faced, not only sexist statements
that reflect the staff's assumptions, but also the question of what to do about
sexism that seeps into copy from a variety of other sources.

As for sexism that comes from within the news staff, critics of media
sexism have offered a remedy—employ more women in writing, editing, and
producing and sexism will wither away. The remedy should be examined carefully, in the light of the fact that a considerable number of the sexist sentences
bear women's bylines.

At the heart of the remedy are some assumptions that may not hold up:
all women are feminists and no men are feminists; women are so thoroughly
socialized as women that no subsequent socializing in the newsroom can over-
ride their self-consciousness as women; women are willing to take the political
risks involved in the mission of rooting out sexism wherever it appears. These
assumptions are misleading and not borne out in reality.

How many male feminists there are in newsrooms or in society at large
is undetermined, but there are men writing letters protesting journalistic sexism to the editor.

Female journalists may well identify more with the "journalistic" part
of their identity than with the "female" part. Working in male-dominated
places requires, or at least encourages, this identity. The most comprehensive
sociological study of U.S. journalists, "The News People" by John W. C.
Johnstone, Edward J. Slawski and William W. Bowman, offers no evidence
that the journalistic values or the media criticisms of female journalists differ
significantly from those of male journalists. Further, although the women
studied had inferior status and lower salaries than men in the profession, the
women as a group had slightly higher levels of job satisfaction than the men.
None of this supports the expectation that women would take the lead against
sexist content, especially the veiled and subtle sort.

Finally, female journalists are in an intolerable double bind if they are
counted on to root out sexism from their organization's messages. Except in
advocacy media, journalistic codes endorse "objectivity" as a goal. The staff

member who continually identifies and complains of sexism in the content is soon perceived as an advocate of feminism and thus disqualified as "objective." (A number of feminist journalists were not allowed to cover the Houston women's conference on those grounds.) The consequences for one's career and one's relationship with associates are quite clear to female journalists. Thus, they hesitate to gamble.

Presuming that news organizations wish to eliminate sexist language and that women staffers can't be held totally responsible for its elimination, what other remedies might work? After nearly a decade of discussion, easy answers elude us. Still, the following suggestions may be useful.

1. Another review of stylebooks might be in order, with additional examples illustrating more subtly sexist language than that shown in current style manuals.

2. Seminars by specialists in linguistics and feminist studies might help staff identify problems in writing and editing.

3. Some "consciousness raising" among staffers may be advisable. If those who must use the style manuals don't understand the motivation behind the changes, that might be contributing to their trouble in applying the "rules." Editors and writers should discuss the reasons that probably underlie stylebook changes:

Sexist language is politically intolerable.

Sexist language can lead to inaccuracy and unprofessionalism.

Sexist language undermines "objectivity."

Sexist language is unethical.

NEUTERING THE COPY

R. Thomas Berner

Last October, an article by Jean Ward brought us up to date on the movement to eliminate sexism in the news. Recently I learned there is also a war of the words in some parts of the publishing world. It happened while I was working on something akin to a grammar book for reporters. Now I fear some editors may value "equality" more than precision.

In the beginning my publisher cautioned me to avoid sexist language. That is, to keep out any discriminatory references and stereotyping.

Thus, instead of *newsman* I used *journalist* or *reporter*—even though the meanings are slightly different. Elsewhere, *councilman* became *council member*. Egalitarian to a fault, I included sample copy with a woman doctor and a woman police chief. All fine with me.

During the initial editing, however, my publisher criticized my use of, say, *the reader . . . he,* and said this must be changed to *readers . . . they.* I was forced to argue that all good writers try to make their work as personal as possible. Only then did the company agree to a compromise: Whenever such a reference is not clumsy, the singular *reader* (and *journalist* and *writer* and any other singular neutral word) should be *he* or *she* on second reference.

The problem became even more visible during the final editing. For example, I had written *a print journalist . . . he.* My copy editor (a woman) changed that to *newspaper* or *magazine journalists . . . they* and thus altered the meaning slightly.

Further, the editor switched pressmen to *press people.* I fought it—after reading that three New York City newspapers had set a deadline for a new contract for Printing Pressmen's Union No. 2. When the union's members vote to call themselves *press people,* then I'll use the expression. Needless to say, I changed *press people* back to *pressmen* and wrote in the margin of my proofs: "This is absurd!"

So was this: I had a sentence referring to a nurse who was "ashamed to take her child with recurring pinworms to a doctor." The copy editor replaced nurse with *mother*—not seeing the irony of the situation. Why would a mother be ashamed? We don't expect parents to be as medically savvy as nurses. Then why should a nurse be ashamed to take a child with recurring pinworms to a doctor? The assumption is, nurses shouldn't have such problems. Maybe that's where the stereotype is.

Similarly I said: "If a journalist has a quote he wants to use, he should display it." It was changed to: "If there is a quote a journalist wants to use, he or she should display it." The clumsy *there is* aside, the emphasis on the sentence was shifted from *journalist* to *quote*—even though I wrote the book for journalists and not quotes.

In this sentence the focus is also on the writer: "Perhaps the journalist has a grammar book that says when a writer converts direct discourse to indirect discourse, he should change the tense of the verb one degree." Although a simple *he or she* in place of *he* would have removed the implied bias, the copy editor write: "Perhaps the journalist has a grammar book which says that when a writer converts direct discourse to indirect discourse, *the tense of the verb* should be changed one degree (my italics)."

In shifting the focus, the copy editor also changed one of the verbs from active voice to passive, even though I advise in the book that good writers avoid the latter because it frequently hides the subject of a verb in an unclear sentence.

Finally, I defined sentence fragments: "A sentence fragment is akin to taking a newborn child away from its mother and expecting the child to survive on its own." The sentence was changed to read, in part, "mother or other caretaker." I explained I could not envision a newborn child with any thing or person but its mother, that biologically anything else is impossible. My editor said I could not cast a woman as the sole provider of a child. "Fathers do it, too," I was told as though I had never watched our children while my wife worked.

Never would I have thought anything could come between a copy editor and his/her dedication to precision. I'm afraid, though, the feminist movement has.

This intrusion offends me not only as a writer but also as a journalist, as one who believes in the First Amendment's principles of freedom of the press and of speech. The Constitution allows some of us to be feminists and others of us to be male chauvinist pigs. It also lets us decide.

Of all the elements of journalism that must be conveyed to beginning journalism students, nothing equals punctuation in difficulty. How can a teacher evoke much interest in a bunch of tiny marks? Animation might help: give question marks and exclamation points little arms and legs and perhaps faces to get them to come to life for bored students. Perhaps a play would do the job better, with different students dressing up as semicolons, quotation marks, and commas?

Three essays in *The Quill* offer their own suggestions, primarily by using humor on a subject that is very serious.

* Hyphens receive the attention of former CBS News writer Edward Bliss Jr. in a November 1980 piece that reviews the misapplication, over application, and lack of application of that mark.

* Apostrophes have their own "plight" as explained by freelancer Richard T. Bray in February 1981: they are "misplaced, displaced, or discarded." Bray teaches journalism and English at Suffolk University in Boston and Regis College in Weston, Massachusetts.

* Punctuation marks need a bit of promotion and they'll be more widely accepted and understood, according to Jack Gladden, Wayne State University journalism professor, in a July/August 1981 essay. Before long, academic articles, advertising campaigns, and even whole courses (Hyphen 101) might result.

BRING BACK MY HYPHEN TO ME

Edward Bliss, Jr.

In Neil Simon's play, "Chapter Two," the male lead writes crime stories under the pseudonym of Kenneth Blakely-Hill.

"Blakely hyphen Hill," he explains.

"Hyphen Hill?" a puzzled character asks.

"No, Blakely-Hill with a hyphen."

Wonderful! Here, finally, is someone who finds a hyphen worth mentioning. Hyphens *should* be mentioned. As each year passes, fewer and fewer hyphens are used. When it comes to compound adjectives, the hyphen is becoming an endangered species like Nile crocodiles and the New Guinea snake-neck turtle.

Nowhere is this omission of the hyphen (where it should *not* be omitted) more prevalent than in advertising. The television commercial says that if I take a certain tablet (name on request), I shall get "12 hour relief." A newspaper advertisement proclaims a sale in Filene's basement in Boston, where—at bargain prices—I am promised "long sleeved dress shirts" and "double breasted suits" by "well known makers of fine clothes." Other ads speak of "all day dining," "all night parking" and "salt free peanut butter at $1.29 a pound." In the news columns are references to "well deserved mention" and "first hand experience." (First experience with hands?)

On the way to Boston I see gasoline stations with "self serve islands," billboards touting "strong tasting" low-tar cigarettes, stores selling "wood burning" stoves. A restaurant next to the motel boasting "year round swimming" offers an "Italian style lunch." One sign, mysteriously, advertises "self storage."

Television titles are notoriously hyphenless. PBS, for example, introduced a series last year called "Non Fiction Television." Gateway Productions was advertising a program called "The 45 Billion Dollar Connection." Most blatantly hyphenless, of course, was the "Six Million Dollar Man."

Omission of the hyphen can be confusing. Take the phrase "first class recital." Was it the music class' first recital or was it a first-class recital, one which excelled? A careless headline spoke of a company's "first rate increase." The reference was not to the first increase in any rate but to a first-rate, appreciable increase in production. Hyphens make a difference.

Here I have a confession to make. For years, the CBS evening news displayed a graph showing the "30 day" trend on the New York Stock Market. It hurt to see this, so I wrote about it to the executive producer. Not wishing to appear to intrude—after all, I had left the show—I posed as an aggrieved English teacher and signed the letter "Priscilla Sedgwick." It worked. The hyphen popped into place, and I experienced not only the satisfaction of seeing a spelling corrected on my favorite news program, but also, for the first time, a wondrous, intoxicating sense of Viewer Power.

On those increasingly rare occasions when hyphens *are* used, they frequently are misapplied. There is no hyphen in Boston Herald American. Nor in New York Herald Tribune, a paper fondly remembered though long gone. In 1968, the NBC Nightly News, in reporting the performance of the stock market, consistently hyphenated Dow Jones. Once more, Ms. Sedgwick took up her pen and wrote to the program's producer, and two days later the hyphen disappeared. Right now I'm looking at a newspaper story about a boy injured in an auto accident. The story says the boy is "the 10-year old son of Mr. and Mrs. Michael Ladd." There is no hyphen between *year* and *old*. There should be.

This mistake is commonplace. The writer senses a need for hyphens but doesn't know one hyphen is not enough. The writer simply is ignorant of the *function* of the hyphen in this instance, which is the amalgamation of three words to form one word, an adjective modifying the noun *son*.

Journalism Quarterly, one of this country's most scholarly publications, carried the text of an important address by James W. Carey, president of the Association for Education in Journalism. Reference is made in the text to a "long run effect." We are not told where this run took place, or what effect it had. All we know is that it was a long run, so it may have been a marathon.

I know this makes me vulnerable to the charge of being a smart aleck. But whatever *did* happen to the hyphen? We need it. Let's find it and bring it back—where it belongs.

THE PLIGHT OF THE APOSTROPHE

Richard T. Bray

Consider the case of the pesky apostrophe.

How dreadful those times when we have to face the need to use this troublesome punctuation mark. And often—too often—the poor old apostrophe gets misplaced, displaced or discarded.

How often have we passed a home in suburbia or the city (urbanites do not seem to be any more sophisticated when it comes to the use of the apostrophe) and noticed painted somewhere over a door the words: "The Smith's?" I should prefer to think that the Smiths live there and that Mr. or Mrs. Smith has not abandoned the nest, taking the children with him/her.

I have seen boldly printed on faculty room doors in high schools—where we have a right to expect otherwise—the following: Teacher's Room. A lucky teacher indeed, with a lounge all to himself.

Journalists too are not immune to the little bugger. Recently on Boston's Channel 4 a lawyer representing the parents of Chad Green, a leukemia victim and center of a court case involving his medical treatment, was identified as "parent's lawyer." His or hers? That same channel, I am sorry to report, succumbs to apostrophe-itis at least twice a week.

Perhaps the infectious apostrophe is most dangerous when writers have to use it's or its. Every semester I have a goodly number of journalism students who are so plagued with the malady that it seems almost incurable.

It's, of course, means it is; its is the possessive form as in "Journalism has its share of apostrophe misusers"; and its' has no existence except as an aberration.

Any reader of newspapers and magazines, unless the apostrophe bugs him too, sees repeatedly such abominations as: boy's (instead of boys') room; Patriot's (instead of Patriots') Day; and Veteran's (instead of Veterans') Day.

Linguists tell us that language is ever-changing and that if the nicer distinctions in the use of the apostrophe are lost, there really is no need to lament. After all, without change we'd still be using the Anglo-Saxon genitive (possessive) form of its which was hites.

Still such a loss would say something about the society that allowed it to happen. That is to say, why have we such a difficult time with the once-convenient little mark that printers used to signal a missing letter? Is it that its use requires a certain fastidiousness and tidiness in an age that sanctified the unkempt and disheveled? Is it that it belongs exclusively to the printed page and is ignored by an audio culture? Or is it simply that the use of the apostrophe is just too damn confusing and perplexing for anyone to bother to get it straight?

Who knows? It still mildly unnerves me whenever I see that the little bugger has smitten another otherwise wholesome American family, like the Jone's.

THOSE #!*&/@? PUNCTUATION MARKS

Jack Gladden

When Edward Bliss issued his well-thought-out plea for the return of the hyphen, I read it with high-level interest. I have always thought the hyphen deserved more in-depth attention that it has received in so-called professional journals.

Richard Bray's comments on the apostrophe weren't quite as inspiring, but then I've never thought that the apostrophe was particularly interesting. It just hangs in there and doesn't really do much.

But after reading both pieces, I started thinking: QUILL may have stumbled on something big. In the last few years, countless articles and books have been written by people who are appalled at the decaying state of the language. The authors cite dozens—hundreds—of examples of errors in spelling, grammar and usage. But very little attention has been given to individual punctuation marks.

The Bliss and Bray articles could be followed by a complete series:
"The Answers Behind the Question Mark"
"The Astonishing World of the Exclamation Point!"
"What's the Ellipsis Trying to Hide?"
"Take a Break With a Dash"
The possibilities are limitless.

If the idea caught on, the series could be used as a selling point for advertising. A theme issue on the ampersand could attract full-page ads from Lord & Taylor, Benson & Hedges, Proctor & Gamble & others.

For academicians a whole new world of research would open up. Soon the scholarly journals would be filled with studies such as "A Content Analysis of the Use of the Semi-colon in Multi-column 36-point Headlines in Seven Midwestern Newspapers from 1948 to 1955."

Journalism schools could develop new courses. Students would be required to take (and pass with a grade of "C" or better) "Hyphen 101" before enrolling in "Asterisk 204."

In time some senior faculty member somewhere, aided by a grant from some foundation, would offer a solution to the problem by developing a system of generic punctuation marks. Such a system would particularly benefit the journalism student who thinks a colon is something his great-aunt died of cancer of.

Writers would no longer have to worry about whether to use a comma, a semi-colon, a colon or a dash. They could simply use a generic pause mark. And a generic end mark would solve the problem of whether to use a period, an exclamation point or a question mark in expressions like "So what.!?"

Whatever happens—it's nice to see that, someone is starting to worry about the mis-use of those innocuous little symbols' that, can destroy an otherwise intelligent piece of writing! *(sic)*

Even Lou Grant had trouble spelling in his early days, if an exchange between the famed city editor and his old boss on a weekly in one of the last episodes of that late, great TV series is to be believed. Spelling truly is a curse for many people. A bad speller can get by in some professions; a good secretary or administrative assistant will clear up such things before it is too late. A working journalist has no such luxury. The need to spell words correctly first becomes apparent in a job interview as a grizzled editor sits there circling the mistakes on the resume before him—yours. Passing that test is nothing compared to the daily grind of having to make sure not only that facts are right but that words are spelled correctly too.

The ability to spell may be something that is born within someone, like a way with math or a knack for music. A bad speller can work on the problem—and should do so constantly if a job in journalism is a career goal. The dictionary on the desk of a reporter should be dog-eared from use. The reporter who doesn't pay much attention to spelling will not be a reporter for long, as Bob Eddy explains in this February 1979 article that includes a test over the 50 most frequently misspelled words.

SPELLING: THE CURSE OF THE WORKING JOURNALIST

Bob Eddy

Every day some 200 million persons in this nation are being bombarded by misspelled and incorrectly used words—in newspapers, magazines, books, public signs, TV commercials, advertisements of all kinds. The presidents of universities, the executives of corporate giants, some of the most prestigious publications in this country solemnly publish misspelled, misused words that would make Noah Webster shudder. Does anybody give a damn about spelling?

The esteemed New York Times on Page 1 told of a man's "principle duty . . ." A fine brochure contained a speech by the president of a television network, commenting on how newsmen should report the doings of terrorists: "Don't phone into the beseiged building just to get the scoop. . . ." A wire service story reported how an American psychologist was "harrassed" in the Soviet Union, and that he was "embarassed."

Such errors are not rare. They assault a reader every day. In Minneapolis, a restaurant advertised "SHERBERTS" in an expensive sign chiseled in glass. At the opening of a new restaurant in Hartford, Conn., the menu contained this line: "The slight-of-hand bartender will make your inhabitations disappear." Tiny fingers, presumably, that prepare drinks that leave you unable to find home. A hand-printed sign appeared last month over a busy newsstand in Wheaton, Ill., informing customers that the price of "Wall Street Jornals" had been raised to 30 cents. "No Dumping Aloud!" read a sign in Wisconsin. A student wrote of "the defunked New York Herald Tribune."

Some of even the most intelligent students majoring in fields of communication are atrocious spellers. At the beginning of school, whether it's in a course on newspaper administration or interpretive writing, I give a 50-word spelling quiz on some of the most commonly misspelled words. Midway in the semester the students get the same quiz, then again in the final class meeting. Each time I take out a $5 or $10 bill. In the first session, the offer is "Anyone spelling 45 of the 50 words correctly gets this bill. Please leave me enough money for lunch." In the second quiz, the offer is for 48 words; in the final session it's for 49 words. I've been doing this for years, and have yet to part with my first bill. (Same result, I might add, with newsmen and women and journalism professors.)

In the meantime, a daily five- or ten-minute quiz on grammar and spelling is given in almost every course. My students are eager to learn; and at the end of the semester, when they are asked to evaluate each course, invariably they give high marks to these quizzes. What's baffling is what I find in reading their comments. "Your 'nuts and bolts' drills are certainly an excellent teaching method." The senior who wrote that wasn't trying to be funny. He is a serious, hard-working Navy veteran. Another student commented: "Very usefull."

If spelling can be taught, and when most students are eager to learn, why are so many words misspelled? No conscientious student, no literate person wants to make spelling errors. None wants to reveal a lack of educational attainment, to appear as a sloppy thinker.

One answer lies in the nature of the English language itself. Mario A. Pei, noted linguist, called spelling "the world's most awesome mess," full of "useless verbal puzzles," and the "most anachronistic and confusing feature of English." Other languages—German, French, Spanish—generally follow more consistent rules of spelling. But in English, one finds four-letter combinations such as "ough," which has at least seven different pronunciations, as in dough, bought, bough, hiccough, rough, cough, and through.

Similarly, we have at least 14 one-, two-, or three-letter "sh" sounds, as in shoe, chaperone, issue, ocean, mansion, mission, nation, pshaw, sugar, suspicion, nauseous, schist, conscience and fuchsia. (That last word, incidentally, the name of a flower or a purplish-red color, usually will win a free drink if you can get anyone at the bar to accept your challenge to spell it.)

The "sh" sounds bring to mind the apocryphal story attributed to George Bernard Shaw. A friend is said to have asked, "Are there any words in the English language, other than 'sugar' and 'sumac,' in which 's' is pronounced as 'sh'?" Said Shaw: "Sure." The redoubtable GBS, a language-lover whose play "Pygmalion" and its "rain in Spain" spawned the musical "My Fair Lady," labored mightily for spelling reform. He urged an alphabet of 40 sounds, instead of the conventional 26 letters, and left his sizable estate for that purpose. To illustrate the incongruities of English spelling, Shaw suggested that the word, "fish," could be spelled "ghoti"—the "gh" as in "enough," the "o" as in "women," and the "ti" as in "nation."

Over the years many brilliant minds have pushed hard for spelling reform. But, in the main, the reformers have gotten nowhere, in part because they have not been able to agree among themselves. One outstanding exception was Noah Webster. His monumental achievement, "An American Dictionary of the English Language," completed in Cambridge, England, in 1825 but not published until 1828, Americanized many English spellings.

Today, if it were not for this thin-lipped, dedicated New England intellectual, we no doubt would be writing "labour" for labor, "waggon" for wagon, "centre" for center, "cheque" for check. He Americanized several other spellings: plow for "plough," ax for "axe," jail for "gaol," mold for "mould," among many. His manuscript, with more than 70,000 handwritten entries, became the dictionary, generally, for the English-speaking world.

Some 40 years earlier, when he was 25 years old, Webster's spelling book was published and proceeded to set an amazing record in sales. The book, popularly known as the "Blue-Backed Speller," sold some million copies a year when this nation's population was less than 10 million. Total sales of the book over the years have been estimated at 100 million copies, second only to the Bible.

Did Americans of Webster's day take their spelling more seriously than do today's generations, brought up in an age of increasingly oral communication—radio, TV, tape recorders? Perhaps. But one must remember that most Americans were illiterate then, thirsty for learning, first from Webster's speller, then his subsequent grammar and reader. The illiteracy of the era is reflected in the newspapers, containing far more grammatical and spelling errors than those of today. Of course, printers then set all the type of hand—and it's much easier to blame errors on a printer than on a computer.

At any rate, reading certainly was much more popular as a leisure-time activity before radio and TV moved in, and, as studies have shown, reading improves one's spelling and vocabulary. Today's average high school graduate has spent an estimated 15,000 hours in front of the TV screen, equivalent to 625 24-hour days, with only sleep taking more of his time. This doesn't leave many hours for reading, and undoubtedly has been a factor in lessening spelling ability.

Another reason cited by some educators for the drop in reading—and spelling—ability is the abandonment for several years of phonics studies. Many college students today, for example, can't "sound out" simple words that are spelled phonetically.

But what is truly shocking is the misspelling in the media. The reader of a misspelled word is inclined to believe the word is spelled correctly. The reader trusts, unwisely, the communicator, unless the misspelling is an obvious error. Even in a teaching manual for a journalism editing course, the city, Pittsburgh, Pa., is spelled "Pittsburg." Only in Oklahoma, Texas, Kansas and California may one travel to Pittsburg.

In a list of commonly misspelled words compiled by an esteemed communications department in a Southwestern university, the word, "permissable," is given. That shouldn't be permissible!

A statement passed out at the 1977 convention of the Association for Education in Journalism starts out: "That is a preliminary report on a program to teach certain aspects of English grammer and punctuation. . . ." An errant secretary, perhaps, but certainly startling in its context.

No one, or very few, will spell all the 600,000 words or so in the English language correctly. One encounters such weirdies (slang) as polissoir (a polishing tool) or dithyramb (a wildly emotional song or verse)—two words, by the way, spelled correctly by youngsters in the national spelling bee. But what about the possessive form of "it," as in "The cat chased its tail."? Many college students, as well as their professors and deans, write "it's." Yet, when I write "it's" on the blackboard and ask what it means, the class choruses. "It is!" So why do they keep misspelling it?

And why "guage" for gauge? "Miniscule" I can understand; the prefix "mini" is so common. Few persons, including some professional writers and editors, know that minuscule stems from "minus." And students who would give their eyeteeth to get reporting jobs on graduation groan when asked to spell hemorrhage. Yet it is so simple to remember the "rrh" syndrome in that word and its many Greek brothers from the medical world . . . catarrh, diarrhea, cirrhosis, gonorrhea.

Here are 20 more words that are misspelled by writers, editors and students too often to be funny: receive, restaurateur, annihilate, siege, seize, category, weird, wield, quandary, supersede, exorbitant, exuberant, chiseler, dispel, colonel, publicly, propeller, lieutenant, recommend, theirs. (And there are 50 more on page 18 to tax one's brain.)

A professor also gets a lot of "alrights," which isn't all right. Oddly, just in the past decade or so, students have been writing "alot" for "a lot," meaning many. It's most puzzling. And among these students, I repeat, are bright young men and women. Perhaps they reflect a remark made by Mark Twain: "I don't give a damn for a man that can spell a word only one way."

A bit of the devil-may-care frontier spirit might be read into those words, and a blithe disregard for the strictures of spelling may account for the atrocities one sees committed against the English language every day. "After all," says the student (usually a D or F grade), "if y'know what I mean, and my story will be edited by some dope on the copydesk, what's a few misspellings, y'know, if I've done a good job?"

This student has probably driven to school past a dozen "GO SLOW" signs, seen TV shows the night before with hucksters proclaiming "the most unique sale in history," and hasn't opened a dictionary in weeks. If he's read the morning newspaper at all, he's probably seen misspelled words. . . . What does a teacher say? Do you tell him that it's as easy to spell correctly, once he learns the spelling, as incorrectly, you know?

It's not surprising that at that 1977 convention of journalism educators, one of the best-attended sessions in the four-day program focused on teaching language skills and the increasing usage of tests to screen students seeking to major in journalism. What's shocking is that these screening tests, usually 100 questions involving spelling, grammar and word usage, are flunked by about half the students, most of them sophomores with 14-plus years of American education—and the passing score often is only 70.

These students, mind you, are the young men and women who intend to become this nation's communicators. Many were editors of their high school newspapers. And half of them couldn't answer two out of three multiple-choice questions on the basics of their native language. And many of them, ironically, seem eager to learn, know, use expertly this beautifully expressive English language that is their heritage.

Perhaps it's too simplistic for today's pedagogy and gadgetry, but a modest proposal suggests itself. Why can't the English teacher, in all grades, give a five-minute quiz each class session on spelling, grammar, word usage? Then spend another five minutes letting the students give their answers and discuss the reasons for them?

Some professors look dimly on such quizzes in college journalism classes. "If the kid hasn't learned it by high school, why saddle the bright student with this waste of time?" they ask. Interestingly, the bright student, even the one who can spell, seems to profit from the quiz discussions just as much as the poorer student does. And, happily, the quizzes seem to stimulate students' interest in words. They begin to choose more definitive, specific nouns and sharper, punchier verbs in their writing, as well as getting "who" and "whom" and "like" and "as" straightened out. Many, checking a spelling, also will look at the word's etymology.

Is this too elementary for a college student? Learning should be pleasurable . . . exciting . . . interesting . . . bringing a sense of accomplishment, new horizons. Bringing out a student's curiosity in words—the bricks with which he must build—sharpens his style and spelling.

Maybe it does take a brave teacher or parent to demand quality work in school these days. A two-year study of Scholastic Aptitude Test (SAT) results by a panel headed by former Secretary of Labor Willard Wirtz suggested some causes for the dismal trend in scores. Among them: homework has been cut in half, absenteeism is overlooked, and high grades are given with less regard for quality. If more educators and parents demanded a quality education, at least for these college-bound youngsters—who are not stupid— perhaps I would not have read these two synonyms for bravery in a class re-write assignment on the award of a Congressional Medal of Honor: "bravity" and "intrepidry."

Written by college seniors.

All right, smarty, so you think you can spell . . .

This is a test. The 50 words on the following page are among the most frequently misspelled. In fact, many people misspell them the same way.

Circle the correct spelling, a or b, for each word. The answers appear on page 76.

It took only a matter of seconds for our trigger minds to arrive at a highly scientific formula on how to score the test. Here's how:

If you get from 35 to 49 of the words correct, you're destined to become editor of your newspaper's crossword puzzle.

Score between 25 and 35 and you'll be promoted to the anchor desk. (But you're on your own after that; spelling will not help build your ratings.)

Get 25 right (that's exactly half) and you'll go nowhere. (To move up the ladder of success requires now that you roll doubles; but you are limited to three throws of the dice and must wait your turn.)

Fall between 10 to 24 and you're relegated to writing obits for the next 46 weeks.

Anything below 10 and you must go directly to the Bergen County Jail.

What if you spell them all correctly? Glad you asked. Achieve a perfect score (that's 50 out of 50) and we'll see to it that you're named immediate successor to William Paley at CBS.

Good luck. But before you start, here are a couple of helpful hints:

1. You may think the words are becoming more difficult as you go along. Your instincts are correct.

2. Don't guess. Not that we'd try to trip you up, but you should know that one of the words is misspelled in both a and b.

Finally, a word of caution: If we catch you cheating, we'll burn your dictionary and remove your cathode ray tube.

1. **(a)** grammer	**(b)** grammar	26. **(a)** liason	**(b)** liaison
2. **(a)** arguement	**(b)** argument	27. **(a)** proceed	**(b)** procede
3. **(a)** supprise	**(b)** surprise	28. **(a)** harrass	**(b)** harass
4. **(a)** achieve	**(b)** acheive	29. **(a)** perseverance	**(b)** perseverence
5. **(a)** annoint	**(b)** anoint	30. **(a)** ecstacy	**(b)** ecstasy
6. **(a)** definately	**(b)** definitely	31. **(a)** antiquated	**(b)** antequated
7. **(a)** separate	**(b)** seperate	32. **(a)** insistent	**(b)** insistant
8. **(a)** desirable	**(b)** desireable	33. **(a)** exhillarate	**(b)** exhilarate
9. **(a)** developement	**(b)** development	34. **(a)** vacuum	**(b)** vaccuum
10. **(a)** existence	**(b)** existance	35. **(a)** ridiculous	**(b)** rediculous
11. **(a)** pronunciation	**(b)** pronounciation	36. **(a)** nickel	**(b)** nickle
12. **(a)** occasion	**(b)** occassion	37. **(a)** oscilate	**(b)** oscillate
13. **(a)** assistant	**(b)** assisstant	38. **(a)** tyrannous	**(b)** tyranous
14. **(a)** repitition	**(b)** repetition	39. **(a)** drunkenness	**(b)** drunkeness
15. **(a)** privilege	**(b)** priviledge	40. **(a)** dissention	**(b)** dissension
16. **(a)** dependant	**(b)** dependent	41. **(a)** connoiseur	**(b)** connoisseur
17. **(a)** irresistible	**(b)** irresistable	42. **(a)** sacreligious	**(b)** sacrilegious
18. **(a)** consensus	**(b)** concensus	43. **(a)** battallion	**(b)** batallion
19. **(a)** accommodate	**(b)** accomodate	44. **(a)** prerogative	**(b)** perogative
20. **(a)** occurence	**(b)** occurrence	45. **(a)** iridescent	**(b)** irridescent
21. **(a)** concience	**(b)** conscience	46. **(a)** inadvertent	**(b)** inadvertant
22. **(a)** commitment	**(b)** committment	47. **(a)** geneology	**(b)** genealogy
23. **(a)** embarrass	**(b)** embarass	48. **(a)** villify	**(b)** vilify
24. **(a)** indispensible	**(b)** indispensable	49. **(a)** innoculate	**(b)** inoculate
25. **(a)** allotted	**(b)** alotted	50. **(a)** dilettante	**(b)** dilletante

This spelling test is provided by courtesy of Editorial Experts, Inc. in Alexandria, Va.

Alternative Reporting and Writing Styles

Based on our conversations with those who are curious about the profession, the image (of an investigative reporter) is somewhat . . . romantic, of cloak-and-dagger types whose lives are highly charged with drama and adventure. 'What do each of you do at night?' asked one interviewer, apparently convinced there was no way the two of us could lead normal lives off the job. "Do you just go home?"

Donald L. Barlett
and James B. Steele

Can the impact of news on individual readers be assessed when writing stories? Alex Edelstein and William E. Ames, both journalism professors at the University of Washington, think it should be and even give it a name—humanistic newswriting—in this 1970 article. Edelstein and Ames review the results of a course they taught on the subject and show why bringing out the human side of stories enhances reader comprehension and understanding.

HUMANISTIC NEWSWRITING

Alex S. Edelstein
and
William E. Ames

CONSIDER three possible leads to the same story:

> *1. The City Planning Commission yesterday recommended addition of an RM 1600 zoning classification to the Seattle Zoning Ordinance.*
> *2. Additional land will be opened up for apartment house and townhouse development if the city adopts a recommendation made yesterday by its planning commission.*
> *3. It may soon be possible for a poor family to slowly buy an apartment with enough room to seem like a home.*

The first is a news report of what happened, stated in technically correct terms and all but meaningless to the reader.

The third lead would be written by a humanistically inclined reporter. It talks about what the event means to people.

The examples were devised by Sue Hutchison, an environmental reporter for the Seattle *Post-Intelligencer,* as a way of illustrating the difference between conventional reporting and humanistic writing. Sue is one of three Pacific Northwest newsmen and women who spent time working at the University of Washington School of Communications on an experimental program in humanistic newswriting.

OTHERS WERE Bill Asbury, former managing editor of the Bremerton (Washington) *Sun,* and Alf Collins, real estate columnist for the Seattle *Times.* During winter quarter the program was expanded to include John deYonge, education reporter for the *P-I,* and Alice Kling, a free-lancer writer. Additional reporters joined the project this spring. The program is sponsored by a grant from the National Endowment for the Humanities.

Edelstein defines humanistic reporting as that which is concerned with the impact of news on the individual. It is individualized and personalized, in the hope that the reader will see common threads of experience between his own life and that of another individual.

"If the reader can identify with another person's experience, he feels less isolated as a human being. He develops a greater understanding of others and becomes more able to cope with events," sayd Edelstein.

Bill Asbury borrowed Sue Hutchison's technique of demonstrating contrasts in lead writing. He collected stories that were written humanistically then rewrote them in conventional style. One concerned a young man who was admitted to a Bremerton (Wash.) hospital after an overdose of drugs and alcohol on Christmas Day. The story in the Bremerton *Sun* began as follows:

> *This is "Dirty Eddie's" obituary. It differs from other obituaries in one essential respect—Edward Charles "Dirty Eddie" Whitmire still lives.*
>
> *He's described as remaining in "fair" condition at Harrison Memorial Hospital, after lying in a coma for 12 days. Yet Eddie, as his friends knew him, cannot communicate and probably is unable even to think.*
>
> *Eddie was a charismatic anti-hero of a large number of this city's youth. But the Eddie that was known by Bremerton's underground drug world is dead, and doctors hold little hope for his rebirth.*

Asbury's rewrite presents the same information and demonstrates a more conventional style:

> *Edward C. Whitmire, 20, has been admitted to Harrison Memorial Hospital in Bremerton for complications following an apparent overdose of a painkilling drug.*
>
> *Friends of Whitmire, whose estranged parents live in Seattle, have told police and hospital authorities that he took heavy doses of methadone, a pain killer, at a Christmas day drug and drinking party at the Bremerton home of one of the friends.*
>
> *Police say Whitmire has been arrested repeatedly on drug charges during the last two years.*
>
> *Doctors list his condition as fair though he is unconscious and being fed intravenously.*

Humanistic reporting is not human interest reporting. The latter stresses unusual or unique qualities of individuals. The former tells how one person is like another, how he shares special human qualities with the reader.

When Asbury interviewed a controversial pamphleteer, he asked an unexpected question. Why four-letter words? The answer gave him an unusual story—and one that told the reader more than Who, What, Why, Where, When, and How.

> *Edison Fisk is 55, an electrician, a social activist, a veteran writer*
> *of letters to the editor, a reader of many books, a flaunter of offensive*
> *placards, a purveyor of abrasive ideas in mimeographed pamphlets.*
> *He has made profanity a kind of avocation. He uses language well,*
> *but he seasons his stronger sentences with vulgarity.*
> *"Most words don't cut it when I'm trying to say how serious the*
> *threat to all life is," Fisk says. He slaps his cap on his knee when even*
> *the profanity seems inadequate.*

As a reporter with an environmental beat, Sue Hutchison is concerned about the rapidly diminishing open spaces, the proliferation of shoddy housing developments, and the need for additional public parks and recreation areas. As a humanist, she is concerned about the effect of suburban spread on individuals. Her story about a retired couple who were forced by high taxes to sell their farm on potential park land to a developer made the problem real to many readers.

A report she wrote on a speech by a humanistically-concerned scientist also centered on people:

> *"To speak of man as master of the cosmos is about like installing*
> *a grasshopper as Secretary-General of the United Nations."*
> *The audience laughed when anthropologist Loren Eiseley said that*
> *in a lecture at the University of Washington. But as he continued to put*
> *man in his place the audience grew restive.*

Alf Collins is a real estate columnist with a special interest in housing. He did a story about a University of Washington architecture class which designed a house around him, creating space to satisfy his individual needs and interests. The story was humanistic and so were the architecture students.

"To some extent we are talking about a new definition of news," said co-author Prof. Ames. "We think this is justified in terms of what we know about the problems of newspapers and the needs of readers. And, working with newsmen, as we have been doing, we think schools of journalism can help develop ideas that will be useful."

Editors and reporters who took part in the initial humanistic seminars raised questions about the meaning and applicability of the concept. There are objections as well as agreement.

"I would guess that we could devote a great deal more space to good things than we do to crime and violence, but you don't remember it," said one newsman. "I go home at night and my wife doesn't say, 'Gee, the neighbors got along swell today.' But if the wife threw her husband out the window, I hear about it."

"It's a matter of availability," suggested another. "It's very easy to find out about crime and harder than hell to find out about love."

While humanistic writing tends to stress positive, constructive aspects of human actions, no distinction is made between "good" news and "bad" news. The essential element is concern for the human qualities of the story.

FACULTY MEMBERS involved with the newspaper seminars suggested a systematic approach to news coverage, particularly for crime and accident stories. One of them asserted:

"People need to know more about trends in crime. Telling them that Joe's Delicatessen was held up yesterday may have a certain value, but it does not help the reader develop perspective about an important social problem. We must think of news also as something that happens over time, not as an isolated incident, unrelated to other events or to other people."

"The more we talked, the better we began to understand each other and the potentialities for humanistic writing," said Ames.

"Many reporters are writing humanistic stories but should do more of them. It may be necessary to give such writing a special designation."

Often such stories deal with small events. Often they humanize a public figure. The newsmen searched newspapers from throughout the country to find examples of humanistic writing. The following is from the Los Angeles *Times:*

> *While working on his State of the Union speech late one night, President Nixon learned with difficulty that there is a right way and a wrong way to light a fire in a White House fireplace.*
>
> *The incident, which produced near pandemonium in the executive mansion, was recalled Friday night by an aide who also revealed that the sight of a Southern California beach littered with empty beer cans put a special punch in the antipollution section of the presidential address.*
>
> *The fireplace episode occurred late last Saturday after a white-tie dinner for William McChesney Martin, who is retiring Feb. 1 as chairman of the Federal Reserve Board.*
>
> *Unable to sleep, Mr. Nixon arose to work on the speech he delivered to Congress Thursday. To do so he walked from his bedroom to the Lincoln Room, where a fire already had been laid in the fireplace, needing only a match to set it roaring.*
>
> *Without bothering to first create a chimney draft by igniting some paper, the President applied the match. He was promptly engulfed in smoke, which in turn set off fire warning devices throughout the area.*
>
> *Guards and aides came running. After some effort they established a chimney draft and cleared the room of smoke. A chastened President returned to work on the speech that was highlighted by his fervent appeal for a cleaner America.*

The humanistic story also can make a broad social problem meaningful by focusing on a specific event. A by-line story by Hilda Bryant of the Seattle *P-I* dealt with two problems—racial prejudice and loneliness.

A small Negro-Indian girl and a vivacious Caucasion single-adult have conspired to reverse the significance of Friday the 13th.

On that day career speech-therapist Barbara Ann Likens and 7-year-old Martha will become a family.

On paper that is.

The unorthodox adoption really took place for Barbara and Martha six months ago when the Minority Adoption Project here brought them together.

July 23rd became Martha's new "birthday" because that was the day she came to live with Barbara permanently. Barbara was her sixth "Mom." The others were foster mothers.

But for Barbara, Martha was her very first daughter, and for a single adult who had spent most of her 36 years independently, the idea of being called "Mom" by a beautiful dusky-skinned child took a bit of getting used to.

Inflation is an abstract problem but its effects are specific. So was this UPI story that appeared in the Washington *Post:*

After years of planning, saving and hoping, Jack and Marie Smith (not their real names) have found that their dream of owning a home of their own is still just that—a dream.

Like thousands of middle-class American couples, they are victims of the ever-rising cost of single-family housing in the United States. Although Jack earns about $11,000 a year and Marie supplements their income by teaching part time, they and their three children will have to remain in their four-room apartment just outside of New York City for at least another year, perhaps longer.

According to a recent report by the National Industrial Conference Board, the price of a new single-family home has risen more than twice as fast as the increase in the consumer price index in recent years.

Or consider this story on the same subject from the *Wall Street Journal:*

There is this married woman in the East who is in love with this airline pilot in the West. And he is in love with her. So they have made plans to marry.

But they cannot start out on a shoestring.

Expenses of a divorce, a wedding, and a new home were to have been paid from the pilot's stock portfolio. Until the market dropped. There are other examples:

While the pilot is postponing his marriage, a 73-year-old Cleveland man is postponing his retirement. A Boston man is having second thoughts about buying a $24,000 Mercedes. The backers of a screenplay have pulled out. And a Chicago executive has ordered his wife to serve cheaper cuts of meat.

The common factor in each of these stories is the reporter's concern for the meaning of the event to individuals, those involved in the story and those reading it. Instead of:

> *The price of a new single-family home has risen more than twice as fast as the increase in the consumer price index in recent years, according to a report by the National Industrial Conference Board. A Spokesman for the NICB said. . . .*

the reporter told his story in terms of people.

These kinds of stories do more than liven the page. They provide vivid pictures of different, human kinds of experience. Through the experimental program, we are trying to sensitize newsmen to the possibilities inherent in the humanistic approach. Not all stories should be reported humanistically. But, if the reader is to understand contemporary trends and events, he must obtain information that means more to people.

Too often the opportunity is missed. Recently the New York *Times* reported the following:

> *Atty. Gen. Louis J. Lefkowitz disclosed yesterday that his office had uncovered 361 Wall Street workers with criminal records—including 14 principals and partners of Wall Street firms.*
> *He added, however, that the findings, in a continuing investigation, indicated that only 1.5 per cent of employees of the securities industry have arrest records against the 4 per cent average found in other industries.*

The newsman dutifully reported the attitude of the Stock Exchange and the fact that the investigation was the result of a new law requiring fingerprinting of all persons employed by Stock Exchange firms. But his final sentence hinted at the real story—what the investigation means to the people involved:

> *Lefkowitz said, however, that the fingerprint check had resulted so far in 54 resignations or dismissals.*

This is staggering in its failure to touch the human dimensions.

In a piece about ghetto students in the STAY tutoring program, Claudia Hansen began:

> *"Two weeks ago I stole $150.00 from an office. And do you know what I did with it? I bought everyone I know an ice cream cone."*
> *A thief who buys ice cream cones: sound incongruous? Maybe not, when you know that the guilty party is a 12-year-old boy named Tommy, a seventh grader at a Seattle junior high.*

Another story, this one about a pre-schooler on his way to a Day Care center, was submitted by Dick Montoya:

> *It is very early in the morning and he is very young.*
> *Despite Mom's persistent insistence he is in no hurry to get out of bed—but he does. He stands ready, but not very willing, to join other children who daily leave their homes for crowded public and private day-care centers.*

A sports story by Mike Mowrer describes a turnout by the University of Washington crew, traditionally one of the more grueling sports available to UW athletes:

> *It's four o'clock at the crewhouse, and University of Washington oarsman Craig Andersen strides into the locker room to dress for turn-out.*
> *He gets ready quietly and deliberately, because it is a blustery, wet day outside, and the rumor is going around that turnout is going to be 15 miles long today.*

Again that common element—concern for individuals.

As the undergraduates began to realize, there is a new role for the reporter in humanistic writing. He must become a better and more sensitive observer. He must abandon his reliance on officialdom for carefully quoted opinion and trust his own judgment. He is still bound by high standards of accuracy, but he no longer must strive for the unobtainable goal of objectivity. Instead, he gets inside the story and makes it come alive to his reader.

In evaluating their experimental class, undergraduates called it the most important experience of their journalism study. The humanistic project gave them new insight into the nature of news and enlarged their vision of a reporter's potential contribution.

The students' feelings were shared by the working reporters.

In Sue Hutchison's words:

> *A reporter comes back from a meeting and tells the person sitting next to him about it. He is humorous or disgusted, lively or bored. But he tells a personal brief bit of the story.*
> *Then he sits down and probably doesn't write anything of what he has just said. Instead he writes a report that is patterned, matter-of-fact and neat. The humor or anger of the event disappears.*
> *A newspaper should be a document of the times with all of the human drama and emotion of those times. It is not a matter of cold lead.*
> *I went from the role of skeptic to that of promoter.*

"New Journalism" is hardly new any more. This relic of the late 1960s and early 1970s was never widely accepted by newspapers, except perhaps in an occasional Sunday supplement piece. Magazines became the home of most new journalists. A few writers thrived on the genre in which fact is presented so compellingly and completely that it reads like fiction. When handled well in the hands of a Tom Wolfe, a Norman Mailer, or a Gay Talese, the articles were like literature. When handled poorly, the technique denigrated journalistic credibility and standards of accuracy.

The best legacy of new journalism in the 1980s is its concentration on new ways to present material and on good writing. *The Quill* has presented a number of articles on the subject since the heady days of the 1970s when new journalism was used more widely than it is now. Although the articles are a decade old they are useful guides to an approach that does credit to both writer and publication if it is handled right.

* In "The Authentic New Journalists" (1971) David McHam, now at Southern Methodist University, reviews the history of that technique and some of the earlier controversies it created.

* In the same issue, George Bailey, a journalism professor at the University of Wisconsin at Milwaukee, presents a debate on new journalism held at a meeting of that school's SPJ,SDX chapter.

* In "From Lippman to Irving to New Journalism" (1972), Dennis Chase, then with the MicGraw-Hill World News Chicago bureau, traces new journalism to its roots, that Olympian statesman, Walter Lippmann.

THE AUTHENTIC NEW JOURNALISTS

David McHam

LOST IN THE hue and cry over activism in the news rooms, participatory journalism and pros and cons in definition of "new" journalism is the simple fact that change has been taking place in reporting and writing in this country in the last decade.

Those who spend a lifetime inside a newspaper office are sometimes the last to notice what evolution brings to their products. The pressures of other considerations do not allow for sufficient time to take full note of developments in related journalism, particularly in magazines and books.

The threat is what veteran news management personnel respond to most readily. Of late there has been a threat, as viewed from the eyes of the traditionalists. It is personified by men with long hair, sideburns and beards and women who'll come to the office in anything from hot pants to ponchos.

Not all these people, mostly young, wearing long hair or ponchos bring with them the taint of activism, although they seem fated by the "birds of the feather" adage. Perhaps there are just as many closely shorn and properly dressed young men and women in news rooms who have adopted something approaching the so-called activist approach.

The young ones may adopt the more participatory attitude out of naivete, poor training, improper motivation, inadequate guidance, lax newsroom discipline and/or a variety of other commissions and omissions.

Older ones reach a point of despair at what they see as inept traditional approaches, imperfect methods and, most serious, the inability—intentional or otherwise—of the press to respond to its readership as fairly and responsibly as it professes.

The tendency in this confusion of people, motives, situation and circumstance is to look for the easy and oversimplified explanation. And often that explanation goes something like this: "So this is the 'new' journalism we've been hearing about!"

But it is not. That is, there is something going on that has been called capital N, capital J New Journalism, but it is not necessarily activist or participatory and it is not necessarily practiced by untrained, inexperienced, undisciplined would-be journalists.

One of the difficulties associated with the development of New Journalism is that no one has written a handbook explaining what it is and how to go about it. (Tom Wolfe later collected a number of New Journalism articles in a book by that name.)

The present state of the art has come about informally, slowly and on a number of fronts. Word about it passes through conversation and discussion among writers and hopeful writers. But mostly New Journalism is discovered through reading and observation and learned by experience and hard work.

There is no such thing as the one example of New Journalism. What or who is included during discussion is determined by point of view. Few or many sources might be examined. Naturally the more writers, magazines and books listed the more difficult becomes the attempt to explain by example what it is.

New Journalism is not alien to newspapers and wire services. The story that won the Pulitzer Prize for Thomas Powers and Lucinda Franks of United Press International on Diana Oughton, the young radical who was killed in a Greenwich Village bomb factory, is an example. So too are many of the works of Hugh Mulligan and newsfeature writers of The Associated Press. And newspapers abound with examples, some not so "new."

But magazines have been the best proponents of the trend and indeed they have had much to do with sponsorship of it through publication of articles that have been reported and written in what may be called the "new" approach.

Esquire was the first and has done more for the new approach than any other magazine. Selected articles from *Esquire* during the 1960s appear in a book, "Smiling through the Apocalypse." Harold Hayes, then editor of *Esquire,* edited the book and wrote an introduction in which he explained how the change took place at the magazine.

Hayes said the attitude "took shape as we went along" and that "any point of view was welcome." Then he said, ". . . but we tended to avoid committing ourselves to doctrinaire programs even though advised on occasion that we might thereby serve better the interests of mankind."

That introduction by Hayes is a must for anyone attempting to get his bearings on the subject. He explains what the writers were trying to do in becoming "central to events." For instance he lists "freedom-riding down South, slogging through the Mekong Delta, marching on the Pentagon, backtracking Kansas killers, running from cops in Chicago and so on." He says that these writers were "keeping witness in the truest sense, and all readers were the richer for it."

There are so many outstanding examples in "Smiling through the Apocalypse" it is not fair to pick out one or two and ignore the others.

But one situation regarding *Esquire* stands out as a point of reference. It involves Tom Wolfe, who was commissioned to go to California "to take a look at the custom car world." What emerged as "The Kandy-Kolored Tangerine-Flake Streamline Baby" is the title story in Wolfe's first collection of his work. In the introduction he tells how he came to write the story in the way he did.

"But at first I couldn't even write the story. I came back to New York and just sat around worrying over the thing. I had a lot of trouble analyzing exactly what I had on my hands. By this time *Esquire* practically had a gun at my head because they had a two-page-wide color picture for the story locked into the printing presses and no story. Finally I told Byron Dobell, the managing editor at *Esquire,* that I couldn't pull the thing together. O.K., he tells me, just type out my notes and send them over and he will get somebody else to write it. So about 8 o'clock that night I started typing the notes out in the form of a memorandum that began, 'Dear Byron.' I started typing away, starting right with the first time I saw any custom cars in California. I just started recording it all, and inside of a couple of hours, typing along like a madman, I could tell that something was beginning to happen. By midnight this memorandum to Byron was twenty pages long and I was still typing like a maniac. About 2 A.M. or something like that I turned on WABC, a radio station that plays rock and roll music all night long, and got a little more manic. I wrapped up the memorandum about 6:15 A.M., and by this time it was 49 pages long. I took it over to *Esquire* as soon as they opened up, about 9:30 A.M. About 4 P.M. I got a call from Byron Dobell. He told me they were striking out the 'Dear Byron' at the top of the memorandum and running the rest of it in the magazine. That was the story. 'The Kandy-Kolored Tangerine-Flake Stream-line Baby.' ' "

What these articles such as Wolfe's and others do is to get into a subject in depth, to look at it with great detail, sometimes from more than one point of view and sometimes with penetrating insight into only one point of view. The mode gives the writer the opportunity to get into a subject, to move around inside it, to look it over and then give that information to the reader.

The articles are not preachy, they do not intend to have the only answer, they do not evaluate the material in terms of right and wrong. The information is there for the reader to look at, to mull over. In the end the reader can make his own decision about it.

Such an approach may not be new. If there is anything new at all it is the trend that has developed. But it is refreshing, especially from the reader's point of view, because he is able to read an article he can think about and discuss. If there is any participation at all in New Journalism it is that of the reader.

More than likely what the writer has failed to include becomes apparent and, at any rate, the reader isn't bamboozled. This is a charge from the staid, strictly-structured, this-is-the-way-it-is method that may quote everyone accurately (if out of context), be balanced and be fair to everyone but the reader, who gets an unclear picture of what is actually going on.

Wolfe referred to this in his introduction to "The Kandy-Kolored Tan-gerine-Flake Streamline Baby" in explaining how he covered a Hot Rod & Custom Car show in New York for the *Herald Tribune*.

"I brought back exactly the kind of story any of the somnambulistic totem newspapers in America would have come up with. A totem newspaper is the kind people don't really buy to read but just to *have,* physically, because they know it supports their own outlook on life."

So there may be some activism in New Journalism, but if there is it is in opposition to the traditional method. And it is loyal opposition. The result is in the reader's favor, as Hayes said. Because of the type of writers attracted to New Journalism, magazines instead of newspapers present the best forum.

ONE SUCH FORUM is *New York* magazine, which got on to the new concept back when it was the Sunday magazine in the New York *Herald Tribune.* (Former editor) Clay Felker and staff did it with a rarity among modern journalism, the successful, independent, weekly magazine that was started from scratch. Well, practically from scratch.

Tom Wolfe may have provided the turning point for *New York*. His "Radical Chic: That Party at Lenny's" appeared in the June 8, 1970, issue and seemed to provide a spark for the magazine. If all this seems to make Wolfe the father of New Journalism it is not intended to. Hayes and his staff must share in that title and Gay Talese has played an important part. Even Truman Capote and Norman Mailer can stand up for bows. But more on that later. Back to *New York*.

A look at almost any issue of the 1970s will bring forth examples. Two articles appearing in the May 3, 1971 issue will serve as cases in point.

Gail Sheehy covered and wrote interestingly about "The Putnam County Witch Trial," a controversy over the dismissal of an elementary school teacher at Mahopac Falls, New York. The article was written from the point of view of the teacher, Kathleen Marcato, and hence was more than a little sympathetic. While it wasn't advocacy, the article did tend to emphasize the incredulity in the situation.

A paragraph from the article points this out: "Her crime was the hanging of a poster on a public-school bulletin board as part of a Christmas display. It was flowered and carried the message: WAR IS NOT HEALTHY FOR CHILDREN AND OTHER LIVING THINGS."

In the same issue Robert Daley gave a vivid portrait of Frank Serpico in "Portrait of an Honest Cop: Target for Attack." What makes this story interesting besides the information contained in it is that *New York* magazine apparently found Frank Serpico, although he was there for anybody to find. Two weeks later Serpico was a guest on the Dick Cavett show and his appearance demonstrated that a writer is able to capture a situation and the personality of the participants better than a talk show host with the major participant there.

This was followed with stories devoted to Serpico in the May 31, 1971 issues of *Time* and *Newsweek*. *Newsweek* said: "The crusading cop came into the public spotlight earlier this month in a story in *New York* magazine. Soon after it appeared, the story's 41-year-old author, Robert Daley, the son of the New York *Times'* sports columnist Arthur Daley and himself a former *Times* correspondent, was appointed to the job of police press-relations director. And Serpico, after eleven years on the force, received the gold detective's shield signaling promotion from patrolman's rank."

Time recounted the story in great detail but without the incidents, the stories and the dialogue that made Daley's account stand out. *Time* also reprinted a picture from *New York* magazine, with credit.

The result of the *New York* story and surrounding publicity has been to focus attention on corruption within the New York City police department and helped spur what *Newsweek* called "the biggest crackdown on New York City police corruption since the Harry Gross bookmaking scandals of the 1950s."

The styles of the "witch trial" and "honest cop" stories were different, but they had things in common: they were well researched, imaginatively reported, they had as many facts as were consistent with the scope of the articles and through the presentation the reader got to know the principals involved. The stories were not necessarily, in the strictest sense, balanced, however, and persons with different points of view might even say they were not fair.

The May 24 issue of *New York* contained 10 letters in response to Miss Sheehy's article. The letter writers were complimentary, they were outraged in the teacher's behalf, they begged the inclusion of additional information and one was critical. The letter said: "It is true that most people held strong opinions on how the case should be resolved, but the difference between us and your reporter is that whichever way we feel, we are willing to respect the other view, believing that most people reached their decision after careful thought and investigation." Then later: "In the final analysis, what you have done is damn an entire community, create a sincere doubt about the accuracy of reporting on difficult or controversial issues and damage the reputation of many sincere people." The writer was a woman who lives in Mahopac, New York.

So, NEW JOURNALISM can be controversial, as is proved by the state of affairs at *Harpers* (in the early 1970s). The best of New Journalism had been wrapped in the package edited by Willie Morris. Without getting into the difficulties Morris and *Harper's* had with each other, suffice it to say that Morris, David Halberstam, Larry L. King, Marshall Frady, John Corry, et al were putting out a product that was an advocate of New Journalism's dream.

The coming-of-age article was one David Halberstam did on McGeorge Bundy in the July 1969 edition. The article gives through Bundy a comprehensive picture of the uses and abuses of political power during the Kennedy-Johnson years and especially details the evolution of the Vietnam war.

Eleven months later Morris' return to Yazoo presented an interesting example of reporting because it involved the soul-searching that few writers must encounter. Morris' earlier "North Toward Home" was another example in book form. His "Yazoo . . . notes on survival," now also out in book form, is so complete it can't help but be balanced. Fair? It is fair to anybody except the reader who approaches it with a preconceived view.

Larry L. King may have been the best showpiece of the *Harper's* of old. His five articles over a year and a half were the kind that caused people who appreciate good writing to meet their friends with a "Did you see the Larry King story on thus and so?"

They were "Confessions of a White Racist" in January 1970, "Whatever Happened to Brother Dave?" in September 1970, "Blowing My Mind at Harvard" in October 1970, "The Old Man" in April 1971 and "The Road to Power in Congress" in June 1971. "Confessions," now in book form, explains growing up in white America in a personal, intimate, frank way that is as sobering as it is revealing. And anyone who can read "The Old Man" without getting a catch in the throat or a tear in the eye is a hard individual.

While the essay and first person approaches may be held in disdain by many New Journalists, Morris (in "North Toward Home") and King (at *Harper's* and in his collection, ". . . And Other Dirty Stories") carry off a mixture of the two in superior fashion. And both can report, as seen in "Yazoo" and in "Road to Power."

On the "About This Issue" page of the June 1971 *Harper's*, King discusses how he went about the task of reporting on the ascension of Hale Boggs as House majority leader and the defeat of Morris Udall. "A lot of cross-checking was necessary: sometimes I'd get a half-dozen versions of the same story or incident, and then have to winnow out something that was a little more than a committee truth. There was always the problem of each politician telling the story so that it would do him credit or show up a rival."

There again is another aspect of New Journalism and in the study of the subject discoveries are made in just such fashion. In all these examples there are aspects of what New Journalism is. But New Journalism is something else, too. It is personal in that it tells about people, who they are and what makes them tick.

Therefore in examining New Journalism it would be appropriate to look at it by looking at the individuals involved, the writers. But what writers to include? For academic purposes, let's include Truman Capote, Norman Mailer, Tom Wolfe and Gay Talese. That omits a lot of people. But these four offer variety, if not the full scope of the field.

Truman Capote?, you say. And Normal Mailer? Why them? Here's why:

Everyone knew Capote was on to something because he told us he was. In the January 7, 1966, issue of *Life,* to use just one reference of many, Capote recounted how he spent six years unraveling a Kansas murder case. In explaining why he, a novelist, did it he said: "I went way out on a limb and risked six years of my life not to get rich but to invent a serious new art form.

"My theory, you see, is that you can take any subject and make it into a nonfiction novel. By that I don't mean a historical or documentary novel— those are popular and interesting but impure genres, with neither the persuasiveness of fact nor the poetic altitude of fiction. Lots of friends I've told these ideas to accuse me of failure of imagination. Ha! I tell them *they're* the ones whose imaginations have failed, not me. What I've done is much harder than a conventional novel. You have to get away from your own particular vision of the world. Too many writers are mesmerized by their own navels."

To quote *Life:* "But, Capote believes, he could have written just as effective a nonfiction novel about a topic far more prosaic. 'I don't think crime is all that interesting a subject,' he says. 'What could be more cut and dried, really, than two ex-convicts who set out to rob a family and end up killing them? The important thing is the depth you can plunge to and height you can reach. The art form I've invented allows for great flexibility that way.' "

Capote's claims to a new art form—the nonfiction novel—aside, he did through intense interviewing and research recreate a story almost as though he were there. The strange thing is he did it without taking notes or using a tape recorder. The prediction by Capote and others that more and more novelists would turn to the journalistic style has failed to materialize. But a few have tried their hand and the idea remains an intriguing one.

ALONG WITH CAPOTE, journalism's greatest steal from the literary world has been Norman Mailer. But since Mailer isn't the kind of guy that people are neutral about, some journalists are ready to give him back to the literati. Some of them don't want him either. New Journalism will take him. It is not a closed corporation. Mailer's contributions have been significant in that he has done at least a couple of things that nobody else has had the foresight— or maybe the talent—to do.

The best example is "The Armies of the Night," which earned him a Pulitzer Prize. Once you get past Mailer's ego—which seems to be his greatest fault as a reporter—you realize that he has captured an historical event with great depth and insight. How else could anyone know what the October 1967 anti-Vietnam march on the Pentagon was all about and what it was like unless he had been there. Mailer was there and he takes the reader there with him in the book. And some of the time the personal references actually help to set the scene.

His "Miami and the Siege of Chicago" perhaps offers better examples of his intuitive reporting skill. His characterizations of Miami and Chicago are classic and he places the personalities there in such a way they tend to take on the character of the cities and the political conventions. Or maybe it's the other way around.

Overlooked by many was an earlier Mailer attempt at reporting on the 1960 Democratic convention in Los Angeles. That effort appeared as "Superman Comes to the Supermarket" in the November 1960 edition of *Esquire*. It is also the lead story in "Smiling through the Apocalypse."

Mailer's "A Fire on the Moon" will have to await the test of history. Some critics loved it, but as many or more detested it. Again, the ego seems to be the flaw. His "The Prisoner of Sex" in the March 1971 *Harper's* did not have to wait as long for judgment, but even the immediate response was mixed.

If Capote and Mailer are the literary specimen of New Journalism, Talese and Wolfe are its shining lights. They are the ones who did it not just once, but over and over again. It would be difficult to select one over the other as the best individual example of New Journalism. Both have done well and they have done what they've done in slightly different ways.

Wolfe, because of his interest in the sociology of the 1960s, because of his incredibly fortunate timing, because of his unusual writing style and because he has emerged as the spokesman of New Journalism, has attracted the most attention.

His published books now number four. Three are collections including the recent "Radical Chic & Mau-Mauing the Flak Catchers." The fourth is the highly interesting account of life with Ken Kesey and the Merry Pranksters. Wolfe's range has been great and it shows he is definitely not mesmerized by his own navel.

His article on "The New Journalism" in *The Bulletin* of the American Society of Newspaper Editors in September 1970 is the most definitive work to date on the subject. (The article appeared in expanded form as an introduction to the anthology noted earlier.)

In the article he discussed " 'saturation reporting,' upon which so much of the New Journalism depends. For years the basic reporting technique has been the interview. You have a subject to write about, so you go interview the people who know about it, you write down their answers and then you recount what they said.

"Saturation reporting is much harder. You are after not just facts. The basic units of reporting are no longer who-what-when-where-how and why but whole scenes and stretches of dialogue. The New Journalism involves a depth of reporting and an attention to the most minute facts and details that most newspapermen, even the most experienced, have never dreamed of. To pull it off you casually have to stay with the people you are writing about for long stretches. You may have to stay with them days, weeks, even months—long enough so that you are actually there when revealing scenes take place in their lives. You have to constantly be on the alert for chance remarks, odd details, quirks, curios, anything that may serve to bring a scene alive when you're writing. There is no formula for it. It never gets any easier just because you've done it before."

TALESE'S WORK pre-dates all the other New Journalism. He was doing it back on the *Times,* as careful readers will remember. Many of the pieces were short, but they had the color, the flavor, the feel of something special in writing. At that time he was also collecting information for "The Kingdom and the Power," the story of the New York *Times.*

His individual works may stand out above anything anybody else has done in New Journalism, particularly his "Frank Sinatra Has a Cold" and "The Silent Season of a Hero," his story on Joe DiMaggio.

While Wolfe uses language flamboyantly, Talese relies on what he calls interior monologue. In a panel discussion in which he, Wolfe and Hayes participated at the Graduate School of Journalism at Columbia in the fall of 1969, Talese noted another difference in himself and Wolfe:

"Here you have in Tom and myself two people about the same age, who in reporting have gone off in quite different directions, although admiring many of the same things, including my admiration for him. But Tom is interested in the new, the latest, the most current; Tom is way ahead in knowing these things, and relays them to those who read him, including myself. What is so contemporary, or what will be. I'm more interested in the old things, the Joshua Logan trying to make a comeback, the Joe DiMaggio become an old hero, how his life is, a Frank Sinatra, who seems to symbolize, at least to me, fame and how a man lives with it. I keep getting off the point. The point was to try to say something about how I got into New Journalism. Or old journalism. Para-journalism is Dwight MacDonald's description of it."

IN EXPLAINING his use of interior monologue, Talese said he was trying to carry New Journalism further. "I rarely if ever will use a direct quotation any more. I'll use dialogue, but I would never, if someone that I may be interviewing, and following around, should say something, I would never quote as an old *New Yorker* profile might quote some fisherman for 8,000 words in a row. Never do I use direct quotations. I always take it out of the direct quotation and use it without quotations but always attribute. And very often, now, if I were interviewing Tom Wolfe, I would ask him what he thought in every situation where I might have asked him in the past what he did and said. I'm not so interested in what he did and said as I am interested in what he thought. And I would quote him in the way I was writing as that he thought something."

These remarks by Talese indicate that even before New Journalism is firmly identified subtle changes are taking place.

While the debate continues over objectivity vs. subjectivity, New Journalists are turning their attention to subjective reality. It is objectivity without passion, to paraphrase Wolfe. He put it this way:

"In most cases the new nonfiction is morally objective—in the sense that it allows the reader to make his own judgments, based on the experience the writer has enabled him to have. The experience is the important thing."

Whether activism in the newsroom is good or bad may not be answerable without the benefit of historical perspective. There's little doubt that it has forced change and much of the change has been for the good. But the excesses of the activists may in the end do more harm than good in insulating "the system" against change.

But one thing is certain. There is a great difference between the indulgences of a naive, immature reporter and the thorough, detailed reporting of the likes of a Gay Talese or a Tom Wolfe.

And that's the difference in activism and New Journalism.

THE 'NEW JOURNALISM' DEBATE

George Bailey

THE CONTROVERSY over "New Journalism" is unlike some esoteric debate over a new drug by a college of surgeons. The product of journalism is public, and journalism's professional policy debates have become public affairs.

Case in point: The CBS AM station in Chicago, WBBM, does all-news programming. Commentator in residence is John Madigan, formerly of *Newsweek,* Chicago's *American* and a television talk show, "At Random." Now Madigan covers . . . no, he uncovers the wonders of politics in Chicago and downstate Illinois. Unlike many broadcast commentators, Madigan avoids light tribute to songbirds and mothers. He is a scrapper and an aggressive and informed interviewer.

One evening (in 1971) Madigan's airtime was journalism on journalism instead of the usual journalism on politics. He noted that Curtis MacDougall of Northwestern University's Medill School of Journalism had been honored by the Chicago Professional chapter (Headline Club) of SPJ,SDX and the Chicago *Sun-Times* had reported MacDougall's speech as approving the "New Journalism." Madigan used that item as a sprinter's starting block to take off after MacDougall. Here is part of his WBBM comment:

> Now I know what's lacking in all these young newsmen and newswomen coming along these days. They're being trained apparently to become participatory journalists rather than reporters. They want to make moral and political and social judgments on their assignments and then take sides. And they want to do it right from the first fire they cover, into the complicated and controversial subjects (like war, race, religion). Never mind getting the facts straight and writing a strong, fair lead and striving for compactness and continuity. Just get out there and participate. For as Dr. MacDougall said, 'Those brilliant young kids are tired of being scoped by Ralph Nader.' The journalism schools need to teach accuracy and honesty and style and balance . . . not personal involvement.

I heard that broadcast. To my satisfaction, the "New Journalism" had never been A) defined, B) illustrated by actual comparison examples or C) resolved as an issue. Now there seemed to be hope: Two prominent journalists had, in public, taken apparently opposing points of view on "New Journalism." And one had all but challenged the other to a shoot-out.

A joint appearance by Madigan and MacDougall was clearly called for. A series of letters and phone calls quickly established that the two had never met, both were willing to expand their views on the topic and the Milwaukee campus of the University of Wisconsin would be a fine location. On May 12 of 1971, then, students and professors in our Department of Mass Communication gathered to hear a debate of sorts—no formal statement of the proposition and no rigid format—on "New Journalism." What follows is an edited transcript of that debate. All errors of punctuation, omission and the rest are mine only. First there is a prepared speech by John Madigan. Next comes an impromptu reply by Dr. MacDougall. Then there are selected interchanges between the two which were recorded during the open discussion session following the speeches. Whether the "New Journalism" was defined, illustrated or evaluated is left to the reader.

John Madigan, *WBBM, Chicago*

There is a danger of presenting an inaccurate story because the reporter or his editor is a participatory or activist journalist. By these I mean personal involvement in a story, not only covering it with a viewpoint, but deliberately working that viewpoint into a supposedly factual account.

If the New Journalism means taking sides on those matters where men have honest and defensible different views . . . those stories involving Vietnam, the draft, the FBI, race problems, pollution, police, abortion, the pill, hunger, welfare, elections . . . and molding the story to substantiate that side, then I am unalterably against the New Journalism.

Invariably the young reporter jumps to the anti-establishment side. Fine. Let him tell it to his wife. But keep it out of his stories.

If objectivity is a myth, fairness is not and is attainable. Give both sides. The essence of most news is still conflict.

Daniel Moynihan in the March issue of *Commentary* writes that "The national press, especially television, has assumed a neutral posture, even at times a sympathetic one, enabling the neofascists of the Left to occupy center stage throughout the latter half of the sixties with consequences to American politics that have by no means worked themselves out." I agree with Moynihan that at times there has been the image of sympathy, but it does not come from neutrality. It comes from activism and participation. I agree that we should not report patent lies by public officials in public appearances without refutation by another public official or by documentation. But if we are supposed to make judgments, who is to make them? The Moynihans or those who disagree with them?

Editors must assign reporters with discretion. Make certain the man is capable of sublimating his own bias. Never permit a crass reporter—as one did in Chicago some years ago—to walk into the mayor's office and ask, "What do you hear from the mob?"

Reportorial crusades and investigations need the prudence of an experienced editor to protect against the personal, participatory eagerness of Dr. MacDougall's New Journalism.

If the New Journalism is neither activist nor participatory but is just the old respected journalism of proper skepticism, investigation and crusade presented accurately, fairly and giving both sides, then I am for it. But if it is something else, then confine it to journals, columns and comments of opinion. And pray God, you Naders and von Hoffmans and Roykos that even with such license you do not begin on false premises, build with half-truths and twist your target's motives.

Dr. Curtis MacDougall, *Northwestern University*

All these articles have been appearing in *QUILL, Nieman Reports,* and *Columbia Journalism Review* on activist journalism, advocacy journalism, participatory journalism, reformist journalism. Nobody defines them. No one gives an example of a newspaper or a newspaperman, except some of those signed columnists.

As far as endorsing any New Journalism, I have been trying to find out what it is by writing to the authors of all those articles. The main source is a 17-page report by the Associated Press managing editor who views the New Journalism with all kinds of alarm but without any definition. I wrote and asked him what he was talking about. Send some examples. Cite some papers. Cite reporters. And the answers I got back are fantastic. They all say, "Yes, I guess we are talking about interpretative reporting." And there is nothing new except the alarm.

This is a complicated world. It is faced with new explosive problems, new knowledge which demands expert understanding and interpretation. Since the end of the war, the atomic bomb, space exploration and now pollution have been the three areas in which everybody has been scrambling for understanding. When I entitled my book in 1938 "Interpretative Reporting," the reviewers howled at the title and never read the book. If you think Madigan gave me hell, you should have heard what I got at that time editorially from all over.

What is objectivity? What is truth? I remember many years ago in Chicago when we were going to open a new subway and it was not ready in time before the election. One of the papers wrote it in this straight way: "Mayor Kelly took a committee of leading businessmen and public officials on a trial run through the new subway." That was it. Period. Another paper in town wrote: "Trying to be of maximum effect in next Tuesday's election, since the subway was not finished in time, Mayor Kelly. . . ." Now what came closer to giving the people the real knowledge of what happened?

I agree with Madigan 100 per cent that coloring the news, editorializing in the news, writing what should be a straight news story into a personal comment, all that is to be deplored. We do not teach that in any school of journalism as far as I know. We never have and I certainly do not advocate it. In my book the best interpretation is presented as being the complete truth, all of the facts.

Objectivity can be defined only in the intention and the purpose of the reporter. If we do not have integrity and honesty, we have nothing.

In every area of life the old order is being challenged. You cannot sit back smugly. You cannot answer it by repression. To feel that the revolt is not going to infiltrate journalism is unrealistic. It has. I would say that any young person today who is not dissatisfied with something is a jerk. He does not know what is going on. His education has been a failure.

If there is anything to this activism business, I am sure they are not my students. But if there are kids who are going out and writing editorials instead of news stories, then I say fire them the hell out of the newsroom fast. But if they are training themselves to someday be real scientists, specialists in their field who will use that knowledge in the public interest, then that is what schools of journalism should be teaching.

(Dialogue)

MADIGAN: In a pollution story I insist that a person should be sent out to cover it not believing that General Motors or Commonwealth Edison are villains.

MACDOUGALL: Fine, as long as they find that out after they have gone out.

MACDOUGALL: A well-trained journalist, just like a well-trained scientist, can control his opinions. I think he has a better open-minded attitude than most scientists who go out with an hypothesis and try to find the facts.

MADIGAN: I am afraid that on matters such as the death penalty, abortion, the war there are many people who are not sublimating their own prejudices or bias.

MADIGAN: Some people believe that in universities and schools of journalism that, whether they are being taught it or not, students are coming away with not a good healthy skepticism but a genuine distrust and distaste for the established political order and any other established order.

MACDOUGALL: I would say that not only on campus, but in all phases of life there is a growing dislike, a distrust against the establishment. It is not peculiar to schools of journalism. In fact a year ago at Medill we were considering resolutions to endorse the Moratorium and condemn Kent State. I argued for four hours and lost. The vote was 17 to 4 against me. At which time I moved that we appropriate special money for a suitable portrait of George the Third to hang in the room.

MACDOUGALL: When you get out of journalism school go get yourself the dirtiest, lousiest job covering police that you can get. Until you have had your nose rubbed into it you are untrained. There are too many going into your work directly out of school.

MADIGAN: I agree.

MACDOUGALL: The public school has failed completely in training how to read a newspaper, how to watch the media. Eighteen-year-olds are going to vote. Well, I am at an age now where I think that nobody should be able to vote until he is 60. He does not know enough. The public schools are not training for citizenship. They are so afraid of controversy that they stop with World War I. I think it is much more important that students know something about pollution and have a chance to debate all these political issues and have an interest in them, rather than to know how many parts 12 divides. We do not have a trained readership. It gets tougher and tougher to be a good citizen as the objects of tension multiply. We all have our own specialties and we are all tired out at the end of the day. People just are not the good citizens that they once were.

MADIGAN: I would buy that. But I hope that from school you come with inquisitiveness, awareness and a desire for involvement in your block, in your city, in your country and in your world. And a person should attempt to read not just one source at any given time. Never just listen to the radio. Never just watch television. Never just read the Milwaukee *Journal.* I will tell you what Reuven Frank, president of NBC News, said recently: "We must know that the news is neither gathered nor given by men or women seeking office or advantage by what they do with the news! Neither gathered nor given by those who think the news is the means to some better tomorrow only they discern." I agree with that. But I think there are many in our business who now think that they are the means to provide some better tomorrow. I believe that it comes into their reporting. And I think that they want to get it into their reporting. And I think a person has to be trained not to let this come into his report.

FROM LIPPMANN TO IRVING
TO NEW JOURNALISM

Dennis J. Chase

I think that the principal distinguishing mark of New Journalistic style is the writer's attempt to be personalistic, involved, and creative in relation to the events he reports and comments upon. His journalism, in general, has no pretense of being "objective" and it bears the clear stamp of his commitment and personality. (Michael L. Johnson, "The New Journalism" 1971).

The idea was to give the full objective description, plus something that readers had always had to go to novels and short stories for: namely, the subjective or emotional side of characters. (Tom Wolfe, "The Birth of the New Journalism," New York, Feb. 14, 1972).

What these articles such as Wolfe's and others do is to get into a subject in depth, to look at it with great detail, sometimes from more than one point of view and sometimes with penetrating insight into only one point of view. The mode gives the writer the opportunity to get into a subject, to move around inside it, to look it over, and then give that information to the reader. (David McHam, "The Authentic New Journalists," *The Quill,* Sept., 1971).

NEW JOURNALISM may be the most confusing appellation of the decade. No one can define it, and the descriptions often seem to cancel each other out. It is objective on the one hand, and subjective on the other. It is one point of view sometimes, and many points of view other times. It is new, says one school; it harks back to Balzac, says another. The new journalists themselves are divided on this, and Gay Talese, a best-selling author who is always linked to new journalism, now says he is uncertain whether he wants to be. "I don't agree with much of this movement," he said recently. "I don't know where I stand."

The intellectual Godfather of new journalism, and of "old" journalism, for that matter, is Walter Lippmann. While he remains the most profound thinker to ever surface in the craft of journalism, it is this attribute—his very profundity—that has made the directions of journalism mere shifts in the wind all coming from the same source. What has followed Mr. Lippmann is simply a long, long line of paraphrasers, who often sincerely believe they are revolutionary and are honestly unaware of their intellectual debt. The new journalists go one better: they are totally unaware of Mr. Lippmann and of philosophy in general.

Mr. Lippmann's seminal contribution to journalism is contained in his 1922 book, "Public Opinion," where he wrote: "The hypothesis, which seems to me the most fertile, is that news and truth are not the same thing, and must be clearly distinguished." The function of news is to signalize an event, he went on, while the function of truth is "to bring to light the hidden facts, to set them into relation with each other, and make a picture of reality on which men can act."

Why can a journalist not abandon this "signal"—news—and get at the truth? Because "his version of the truth is only his version. How can he demonstrate the truth as he sees it? He cannot demonstrate it any more than Mr. Sinclair Lewis can demonstrate that he has told the whole truth about Main Street." Everyone, says Mr. Lippmann, sees the world through "subjective lenses."

It is this divorce of news and truth that has captured the new journalists. Of course, the "old" journalists had long been proponents of this. Traditionally "objective" reporters are content with reporting "facts" (i.e. news) in a subjective (i.e. "he-said") style that permits the expression of *anything*—without regard for its truth or falsity—as long as it can be attributed to a prominent source. Every politician—including that master, Sen. Joseph McCarthy—has realized this, and therefore has always been the controller of the press (Spiro Agnew notwithstanding). The premise operating in traditional journalism is: reality is not what is, but what people say it is. In this system, "news" does not have to be true, but only *attributable*.

The new journalists have accepted the identical dichotomy, with a few extra trappings. There are many facets to new journalism, but one stands out as its hallmark and is borrowed from the novelists: the ordering of content to create an impression that is closer to "truth" than a mere recital of "facts." The logic is that the sensation one feels at the end of an article is more important than any means used to get there. This technique can involve the use of "points of view" (of several characters, of the author, or a combination), composite characters, telescoping time intervals—anything, as long as the impression is a "true" one. Notice that this system accepts the identical Lippmann-inspired premise that directed the "old" journalists—news and truth are considered dichotomous. The only thing "new" is that the current crop of journalists emphasizes the latter.

It becomes clear why the *National Review* "secret papers" hoax, *Esquire's* phony cover photo of Howard Hughes, and Tom Wolfe's "anti-parody" of *New Yorker* magazine are all examples of new journalism. They each involve a concern with the over-all impression of the reader rather than with the validity or invalidity of the content. After his hoax, William F. Buckley Jr. excused the forged papers in his *National Review* magazine by saying they were "inherently plausible," though not true. Like the novelist, it was an impression that Buckley was shooting for. In this respect, Clifford Irving could be considered a new journalist, points out Renata Adler, former New York *Times* movie critic. The logic is obvious: though Irving lied about his talks with Howard Hughes, the over-all impression in his phony "autobiography" was plausible and could very well be correct, i.e. what Hughes might have written in a true autobiography. "What you're trying to understand is how a situation works," one editor has said, and any means used in this regard is mere "convention."

While the new journalists would loathe any association with *Time* magazine (what could be more "establishment" than *Time*), in fact, the meshing of techniques of fiction and journalism is a *Time* trademark. The ordering of content to "tell a good story," as one new journalist described it, is a characteristic not only of *Time* but of any medium designed for a mass audience, and is always justified as a device to reach the "truth." But Dwight Mac-Donald points out: "How can *Time* get very close to reality when every story has to be tailored and tortured into a little drama, with an angle, a climax, an arresting lead and a 'kicker' at the end?" So it is with new journalism.

Even the predilection of *Time* for the chic, and for the momentary fad or cult, is copied by the new journalists, whose subject matter often is centered in personalities rather than issues. (Pauline Kael, the movie critic, has said she hopes the new journalists stick to these "light" matters because that is all the technique is suited for.) As one author wrote of *Time,* new journalism "contorts human experience, snuffing out its complexity and tidying up its loose ends for an audience which has, after all, come primarily to be entertained. . . ."

The news-truth dichotomy finds a variety of expressions, but they all amount to the same thing. Mr. Lippmann himself, later in his career, made the quite valid point of debunking the distinction between "opinion" and facts. ". . . the old distinction between facts and opinion does not fit the reality of things," he wrote. "No clear line can be drawn where the work of the reporter and correspondent ends and where the work of the editorial writer begins." This is true: opinion—that is, judgment—is implied in every choice we make. This set the paraphrasers off on a whole new thought: now they encourage "interpretation" in news stories, which means: opinion. However, still left out of both Mr. Lippmann's later ideas and the paraphrasers' call to interpret is an accurate placement of truth in this system—of what distinguishes a valid opinion from a lot of wind, and with which a journalist should be concerned.

The news-truth dichotomy is a false one. News is an important or potentially important change in the status quo that can be verified or judged independently by journalists. Truth is "correspondence with facts or with what actually occurred" ("American Heritage Dictionary"). Truth is an *attribute* or *property* of news. The two are related as height, weight and width are related to the concept "solid;" remove any of those properties and you no longer retain the concept; the concept is defined by its attributes. Just so, there can be no such thing as "untrue news;" if something is untrue, it cannot, by definition, be news.

But there is another objection to all this, once again borrowed from Mr. Lippmann. News, he said, is the tip of the iceberg, only part of the "whole" truth which cannot always be seen or reported by a journalist. Do you know the answer to that? It was provided by Mr. Lippmann in another context: "The theory of the free press," he wrote, "is that the truth will emerge from free reporting and free discussion, not that it will be presented perfectly and instantly in any one account."

The error, once again, is the false dichotomy. Only through "news," or facts, is a vision of the "whole" truth possible. In this instance, news becomes the *means* to see the broader truth. Any compromise of the integrity of news constitutes a short-circuit, a corruption of the part, and therefore of the whole as well.

There is a basic fallacy underlying this conception of news and the whole truth. Jacques Barzun has defined it as "preposterism," or putting the result at the beginning. This is the error of the "futurists" who reason that since the future will soon be the present, it can be treated exactly as if it were the present. The new journalists are on similar ground when they declare, in effect, that they will convey what they know to be true, the "whole" truth, without serious regard for the evidence on which this impression is based. The dichotomy is at work again, upending the relationship between news and truth and putting the result (the whole truth) at the beginning.

As a matter of fact, the concept of "whole truth" is a curious one. On the one hand, it is an obviously inflated term, impossible for any man—much less a working journalist—to achieve, a floating abstraction in some Platonic world which, by its nature, is closed to man. As such, it is a meaningless term: who but God can know the *whole* truth, and who would expect it of anyone?

But there is another possibility. One of the keys to new journalism is its emphasis on feeling—specifically, on a feeling evoked in the reader. All may be sacrificed to this. Truth, for the new journalist, is synonymous with feeling; it is intuitive, mystical, and more reliant on a sense than a syllogism. Facts are downplayed: "He (the new journalist) embraces a fictional element inevitable in any reporting, and tries to imagine his way toward the truth," says one writer. Further, errors in knowledge are treated as the inevitable error *of* knowledge.

What does it mean? In this respect, it is worthwhile quoting one "underground" journalist at length:

> We were not sticklers for accuracy—neither is the underground press in general, so *be advised*—but our factual errors were not the product of any conspiracy to mislead the young . . . *Facts are less important than truth*

(my italics) and the two are far from equivalent, you see; for cold facts are nearly always boring and may even distort the truth, but Truth is the highest achievement of human expression . . . Now, let's pick up a 1967 copy of Boston *Avatar,* and under the headline "Report From Vietnam by Alexander Sorensen" read a painfully graphic account of Sorensen's encounter with medieval torture in a Vietnamese village. Later, because we know Brian Keating, who wrote the piece, we discover that Alexander Sorensen doesn't exist and the incident described in Avatar, which moved thousands, never in fact happened. But because it has happened in man's history, and because we know we are responsible for its happening today, and because the story is unvarnished and plain and human, we know it is true, truer than any facts you may have picked up in the *New Republic* . . . All we say: *tell the truth, brothers and let the facts fall where they may* (my italics) . . .

If the new journalists are confused, so was their Godfather. The goal of journalism, Mr. Lippmann wrote, should be "to arrive at that balance of opinions which may most nearly approximate the truth." Nowhere, however, is there any indication that this truth exists, or that it can be known by those with "subjective lenses." Also, it is tempting to ask the embarrassing question of how Mr. Lippmann came to know his truths (or approximations) with *his* subjective lenses. And what claim, if any, can be made as to the validity of any statement in "Public Opinion"?

In fact, Mr. Lippmann has opted for traditional "objective" reporting: journalists can only judge the reliability of sources, not of the news itself. "The news," he wrote, "is not LENIN DEAD but HELSINGFORS SAYS LENIN IS DEAD."

Mr. Lippmann has left us an imperfect legacy, and the current confusion among new and old journalists is the result.

Objective evidentiary journalism—reporting truths based on demonstrated evidence—is possible. Contrary to Mr. Lippmann's claim although there is often disagreement on these matters, this is a problem for journalists, not a characteristic of journalism. All any honest journalist can do is respond in the manner of author Ashley Montagu, whose preface to one book reads:

> This is not a work based on the author's opinions. What I am trying to say in this book is that the evidence set out in it represents the facts of nature. Anyone who desires to argue with the facts of nature should not be intimidated by such a statement. On the contrary, he should be encouraged to doubt and to question, for most people have a way of mistaking their prejudices for the laws of nature. I do not claim to be exempt from this particular frailty. None of us is. The facts set out in this book, however, are either true or false. If it can be shown that any of them are questionable. I welcome the evidence. To my knowledge no one has thus far been able to produce such evidence.

Rather than a new concept, new journalism represents another variant on an old theme. New journalism is dead-end reporting because it is non-credible reporting. It is significant that the cast of new journalists is made up largely of novelists (Truman Capote, Norman Mailer, Gail Sheehy) who want to mesh the two disciplines—fiction and journalism—and who are totally unmindful of any distinctions between these disciplines. But as I have shown, the premises of both new and old journalism hark back 50 years to Mr. Lippmann, who set the trend in journalism as philosophers always do for everything.

It is philosophy that has divorced news from truth, and the result, as poll after poll has indicated, is a drop in media credibility. The connection is obvious, and the solution is to unite news and truth, to stop publishing the lies of official sources and the unvalidated opinions and doctored stories of the new journalists, and to allow into our journals only demonstrable truths that can be independently verified.

After the profession got over its fling with new journalism, it turned its attention to a new fad, investigative reporting. Another argument began almost immediately between those who consider all good reporting investigative reporting and those who had suddenly found a cause and a need to create whole investigative units in their news rooms. After the Watergate scandal was pieced together by reporters from the Washington *Post* and then the staffs of the *New York Times,* the Los Angeles *Times,* and other newspapers and magazines, the interest in investigative reporting increased greatly.

Publications and television stations sent reporters to special courses, financed investigations into local wrongdoing, and then gave wide play to their findings. The results were mixed: widespread corruption discovered and eliminated in some parts of the country on a scale not present since the muckrakers of the first years of the century; in some cases, minor infractions overplayed and sensationalized to an extent that the reporters and editors involved were guilty of the same kind of excess they were printing and broadcasting. Some publications and stations got burned in their early forays into investigative reporting and have pulled back on the techniques. Others are continuing it more carefully.

In a March 1977 article, Donald L. Barlett and James B. Steele of the Philadelphia *Inquirer* reveal the essence of good investigative reporting—more painstaking labor and drudgery than cloak-and-dagger glamour and dramatics. "If there is a rule to be gleaned from that experience," they write, "it is the precept most of us learn or should have learned in our earliest days as reporters: never assume."

In 1981, Ron Lovell wrote a profile of Jerry Uhrhammer, president of the Investigative Reporters and Editors and an investigative reporter at the Eugene, Oregon *Register-Guard.* Uhrhammer, who has since moved to the Riverside, California *Press-Enterprise,* advocates following what he calls the "paper trail" of documents.

SO MUCH FOR THE GLAMOROUS LIFE
OF AN INVESTIGATIVE REPORTER

Donald L. Barlett
and James B. Steele

In the spring of 1972, the two of us trudged up a narrow, wooden stairway at the rear of Philadelphia's labyrinthine City Hall to an isolated alcove nestled under one of the building's great domes.

There, in row after row of brown, aging, legal-size file folders, stacked seven to eight feet high on dusty metal shelves above a concrete floor, was the record of violent crime in Philadelphia for the last quarter century.

Occupying an aged, wooden desk and two disabled chairs, we began to read, take notes and systematically extract information from the files on murders, rapes, robberies and assaults which took place in Philadelphia during one year and how the city's criminal justice system dealt with those cases.

For nearly six months, we repeated this ritual: arriving about 9 a.m. each day to begin work, taking a brief luncheon break at 1 p.m., then returning to our secluded garret for a few more hours of research. Late in the afternoon, we would walk the four blocks north to the Philadelphia Inquirer building to study the day's cases, type notes on the more interesting ones and jot down those that might require a follow-up.

Such is the glamorous life of an investigative reporter.

Based on our conversations with those who are curious about the profession, the image is somewhat more romantic, of cloak-and-dagger types whose lives are highly charged with drama and adventure. "What do each of you do at night?" asked one interviewer, apparently convinced there was no way the two of us could lead normal lives off the job. "Do you just go home?"

Actually, for most investigative reporters, especially those of us who cull material from voluminous public records, the work is anything but dramatic. It requires weeks, indeed months, of painstaking labor which can only be classed as drudgery. It is slow, tedious, often boring work that no amount of Hollywood ingenuity could make exciting.

When we write of the tedium of the work, we mean only the actual physical process of sifting through mounds of dry, initially baffling documents and statistics. By contrast, the results of that labor can be and often are quite dramatic.

For two who specialize in this field, public records reporting has a special appeal. It fulfills one of journalism's traditional roles, that of acting as a watchdog over public officials. But secondly, and perhaps more important in this era of ever-greater governments, it enables reporters to monitor institutions which have such a profound effect on our lives.

Another appeal is that public records offer virtually an endless spectrum of areas to explore. Documents exist on a surprising number of subjects; and, in our own case, we have carried out lengthy investigations ranging over a wide field, from the federal government's mishandling of ghetto housing programs to the origins of the energy crisis.

Documents should by no means be viewed as a replacement for interviews. They supplement each other. But by analyzing the record first, a reporter can ask more knowledgeable questions and know whether the person being interviewed is telling the truth. Records thus become, among other things, an important check on the veracity of a source.

At no time was that point driven home to us more forcefully than during our months-long investigation of Philadelphia's criminal courts.

Like many other big-city court systems at the time, Philadelphia's was rife with opinions on the merits of various judges. With crime in the streets rising, the courts had become a frequent and unwilling target for "lenient judge" barbs by the mayor and district attorney.

In our investigation, we did not set out to either prove or disprove that theory. We set out only to develop hard data on the judges' disposition and sentencing practices by studying literally hundreds of cases handled by the most active criminal court judges during one year.

The data we developed on individual judges did not always square with the conventional wisdom around City Hall, which had neatly pigeon-holed judges into "lenient" or "tough" categories, often for political reasons.

For example, one judge, a political foe of the district attorney, had long been accused by the prosecutor's overzealous assistants of being soft on criminals. If pressed to support their charge, they would eagerly cite a handful of her rulings to buttress their claim.

Naturally, this judge was one of those whose cases we studied. As the months passed, a picture of the judge began to unfold that was somewhat different from the one drawn by the court's knowledgeable sources.

Far from being lenient, the judge was, if anything, tough. Though slightly more likely to impose probation than a jail term compared with other judges, the jurist imposed much stiffer jail sentences than her counterparts.

Arriving at that conclusion took literally months of work slowly reading and recording information about more than 1,000 criminal cases. As much as we would like to dramatize the procedure, there is just no way to do it. In order to see the big picture, we were first forced to find all the little pieces that comprised it, and there were no shortcuts.

Moments of Bliss

Occasionally, though, there are times when a dramatic finding almost jumps out of a document, in one of those rare moments of bliss that seem to justify the long, trying hours bent over the records.

This happened to us not long ago during a lengthy investigation of the American foreign aid program. As part of the investigation, we made a formal request of the State Department to review the files for a major U.S.-backed housing project in South Korea.

After waiting several weeks for clearance to see the documents, we were finally led into a small office at the State Department by one ill-at-ease functionary who directed us to a long table piled high with bulging files.

For a week, we sifted through them. Slowly, a picture of waste and mismanagement began to emerge from the bulky record. Then, on our last day, we came across a document tucked into the files which illustrated dramatically just how far the housing program had strayed from the goals set by the U.S. Congress.

Supposedly built for Korea's poor, the houses were nearly all occupied by bureaucrats and army officers in the employ of South Korea's dictatorial president, Park Chung Hee. Rather than serving as a symbol of United States concern for the downtrodden, the Korean homes had been used by an autocratic ruler to reward those who helped him enforce his anti-democratic rule.

Usually, findings emerge much more slowly and much less dramatically. Our oil industry investigation is a case in point.

Like most of our studies, it began by an extensive reading and copying of public documents. We spent untold hours in the public records room of the Securities and Exchange Commission in Washington copying annual reports, financial records, registration statements and other business documents relating to America's major oil companies.

After returning to Philadelphia with hundreds of pages of copies stuffed in our briefcases, we sat down at our desks at the Inquirer and began to study the reports, extracting statistics which we felt might help us to assess the companies' operations over the last 20 years. On detailed, hand-drawn charts, we entered figures relating to sales, oil refining and exploration in the United States and abroad.

This process went on for days, during which time we never encountered a single entry in the documents that compared in impact to the Korean housing report we had uncovered at the State Department. But gradually, as our charts began to fill up, we were able to see certain major trends underway in the international oil industry, and they were far more significant than our Korea finding.

Our charts revealed a fascinating metamorphosis in the oil companies' operations. From being largely, U.S.-oriented corporations in the 1950s, they had been transformed into truly multi-national corporations by the early 1970s, expanding abroad at a much greater rate than in the states. Their failure to invest here in recent years was one reason for an acute shortage of refinery capacity which aggravated the 1973 oil shortage.

As interest in public records reporting has risen, a number of publications have appeared which provide helpful guides to the vast number of sources of public information at the federal level. These are long overdue, but one should not place too much faith in them.

They should be taken for what they are—a useful tool—but by no means regarded as the last word on the subject. No such publication will ever exist because the subject is too vast to catalogue. Records are always changing and new documents are always appearing.

The only technique for finding all the documents which might exist on a subject is the old tried and true technique of reporting: ask questions, and lots of them. Each investigation must be tailored to the subject under study.

In every investigation we conduct, we find new sources of public information that we did not know existed.

While researching one story about the growing controversy over whether to route a proposed natural gas pipeline from Alaska's north slope through that state or Canada, we became curious as to why one natural gas company in Texas seemed to be gaining influence at the Department of Interior as an advocate of the Alaska route.

While rummaging through Federal Power Commission records, we came across an FPC rule requiring all major gas companies to file an annual report listing, among other things, fees paid to major law firms representing them in Washington.

When we called for the annual report of this particular company, we recognized immediately an influential name. It was the law firm of Mudge, Rose, Guthrie & Alexander, the former law firm of then President Nixon and former Atty. Gen. John Mitchell.

A Deadly Practice

If there is a rule to be gleaned from that experience, it is the precept most of us learn or should have learned in our earliest days as reporters: never assume.

Making assumptions can be a deadly practice in public records reporting. By assuming where records might or might not be found, and by not testing that assumption, one runs the risk of ruling out or underestimating potentially vital sources of information. Sometimes they show up when you least expect them, as in what happened to us with one Antonio Orlando.

In the winter of 1974, after picking up sketchy reports indicating the Arab oil cutback was not as drastic as announced by Middle East oil producers, we expanded our oil investigation to Europe.

On the journey's last leg, the story took us to Genoa, Christopher Columbus's home town and Italy's leading oil port. To accurately measure the impact of the oil cutback, we hoped to obtain statistics from the Genoa Port Authority on the volume of crude oil imported during the months of the Arab cutback.

Having experienced considerable difficulty in the states securing up-to-date oil import figures from major U.S. ports, we were dubious about being able to obtain similar data from a foreign port. Still, we felt it was worth a try.

Buried deep in the basement of the Genoa Port Authority's headquarters, a 12th Century masterpiece of a building which was once Italy's first bank, we found a young, genial researcher for the port, Antonio Orlando.

When our interpreter raised the subject of oil statistics, Orlando displayed no hesitation in rising from his chair and happily pulling out stacks of reports which documented the exact volume of oil imported into Genoa for each month over the previous two years.

Spreading the documents out on a long table in Orlando's Spartan little office, we could see after a quick tabulation that Genoa had been untouched by the alleged oil shortage. Imports were up 19 percent during the months of the "cutback" compared with the same period the year before.

Did Orlando and the port authority realize the significance of the statistics?

"But of course," he smiled. "If you ask me, a lot of people have been playing a great deal on the Arab embargo to close off the taps of petroleum and get an increase in prices.

"As you can see," he said, motioning to his records, embossed with the purplish official seal of the port, "there is no shortage of oil here."

Summaries of Five Series by Barlett and Steele

CRIME AND INJUSTICE

A seven-month, seven-part investigation of the operations of Philadelphia's criminal courts. The investigation disclosed broad patterns of discimination in the administration of justice: robbers were more likely to be sent to jail than rapists, persons under 30 were more likely to receive jail terms than persons over 30, and blacks who committed violent crimes were more likely to receive longer jail terms than whites who were convicted of similar offenses. The investigation, in which more than 1,000 cases were studied, was built around the first comprehensive computer study of a criminal justice system ever made by a newspaper.

AUDITING THE IRS

A six-month, seven-part study disclosing the IRS's annual failure to collect billions of dollars owed the U.S. Treasury and the Treasury's adoption of tax enforcement policies favoring the wealthy. In addition to documenting the gradual erosion of IRS tax collection efforts, the series focused on the cases of high-income taxpayers who had successfully escaped payment of millions of dollars in taxes owed the government.

THE SELLING OF AN OIL CRISIS

A seven-month, multi-part study on the energy crisis in 1973. The series documented the expansion of the American oil industry abroad at the expense of the American consumer and longstanding federal mismanagement of oil policy matters by the federal government. Ranging from the oil fields of Texas to the oil capitals of Europe, the investigation disclosed, among other things, that at the same time American oil companies were accusing American consumers of being energy wastrels, they were urging Europeans and Asiatics to use more oil.

FOREIGN AID: THE FLAWED DREAM

A seven-month, six-part investigation of the $9-billion-a-year American foreign aid program. In an investigation extending from Bangkok, Thailand to Lima, Peru, the series found that the American aid program was punctuated with profiteering, waste, corruption and deception, and was often aggravating the very problems it had been enacted to help solve.

THE SILENT PARTNER OF HOWARD HUGHES

A seven-month, seven-part investigation of the relationship between the late recluse's business empire and the federal government. Contrary to the image of Hughes as an enterprising capitalist, the series showed that his organization rests mightily on the federal government and is nourished by federal dollars. Since 1965, the series disclosed, Hughes's companies have received more than $6 billion, or $1.7 million a day, in contracts from nearly a dozen different federal agencies and departments.

JERRY UHRHAMMER IS IN THE FOREFRONT OF INVESTIGATIVE REPORTERS. HERE'S HOW HE DOES IT

Ron Lovell

Jerry Uhrhammer first heard about the story when a local television station did a number of stories on the same subject. A former county commissioner in his last year in office had engineered a swap of county owned land to real estate developers. They immediately sold the property to others at a half-million dollar profit.

Was there something unusual about the transaction? Uhrhammer, then investigative reporter for the *Eugene* (Ore.) *Register-Guard* and president of the Investigative Reporters and Editors (IRE), decided to dig into the land deal in February 1979 to find out.

"The real estate entrepreneur died several months later," recalls Uhrhammer. "He was the only one who knew everything. His death made it all tougher."

That source gone, the reporter turned to what he calls "the commissioner's financial trail."

"I tracked the real estate transaction by going through the deeds and mortgages in the county recorder's office," he continues. "In four years in public office, the commissioner had gone from a $25,000 home to real estate valued at $250,000, including two condominiums."

Uhrhammer persisted and soon put together the reasons why the commissioner had done what he had apparently done. "There had been political contributions," he says. "I got copies of campaign contributions and expenditure reports and followed that up. He had gotten a good deal on the two condominiums and was loaned money at little or no interest. He had gone on a trip to Reno and the real estate man had given him a job after he got out of office."

By July, Uhrhammer was ready to write the first draft, but was still bothered by one aspect of the story. "I really didn't have it all put together," he says. "I needed the final pieces so I went back to my real estate source. Did the commissioner have knowledge of the fact that the land was to be resold immediately? 'Yes, he did.' The source had heard the real estate entrepreneur call the commissioner to make sure the deal had gone through."

The source had not heard the commissioner's end of the conversation, but her knowledge was enough for Uhrhammer. He had determined that the commission knew the property was about to be resold and failed to inform his fellow commissioners before they approved the original sale. "That was the key thing," he says. "The commissioner apparently had knowledge. Then the story fell together beautifully. I went to the former commissioner and the real estate developer. Both were cooperative. I had two interviews with the former commissioner. In the second one, he admitted it looked 'messy'."

The *Register-Guard* ran a series of articles on the land deal and the commissioner beginning in July 1979. The former commissioner was indicted by the county grand jury for official misconduct in October 1979, following a three-month investigation. He was tried and convicted a year later and is now in prison.

In another situation, about bogus credits and other scandals revolving around the University of Oregon football team, Uhrhammer says that luck more than his abilities as an investigative reporter brought a big story with national ramifications to his attention.

He had been working on one aspect of the story in mid-December 1979 when the scandal broke in New Mexico as part of a larger gambling investigation. A Dallas newspaper mentioned that Oregon and Oregon State football players were involved, and reporters from Dallas called the sports department. After the university conducted what Uhrhammer considered an all too perfunctory one-day investigation of the matter, the reporter went to work.

His luck came in late January 1980 when another athlete came into the newspaper office to complain that another player had burglarized his apartment and the athletic department had done nothing about it. "He also told me about free bogus credits his friend had gotten from a school in Los Angeles and I took it from there and it blew wide open," says Uhrhammer.

These two stories and Uhrhammer's handling of them exemplify three important requirements of investigative journalism: a reporter with experience, ability and keen intuition; solid stories that bear deep exploration; and a newspaper with the resources and willingness to support such a long-term endeavor.

Uhrhammer has been the newspaper's full-time investigative reporter since 1974, but has been doing such stories "on and off" since 1959 when he looked into the obscenity business in the city. "I've always considered investigative reporting as part of whatever beat I was assigned to," he says. "If something comes up on your beat, you dig into it."

Like many other pioneers in his specialty, Uhrhammer was doing what he was doing before it had a name or so much national publicity. The work of reporters on the *Washington Post* and other publications who pieced together the complex story of Watergate that downed a president created the legend of the investigative reporter as American folk hero. Such thinking embarrasses reporters like Uhrhammer who are used to doing their jobs, no more, no less—and with no theatrics.

In 1976, Uhrhammer discovered that other investigative reporters, equally single-mindedly and obscurely, were working all over the country. One day in his mail box at the office, he found a flyer announcing the first convention of a new, year-old organization called Investigative Reporters and Editors. He was immediately interested in attending but found the newspaper could not afford to send him. He decided to pay his own way. "That was the best money I ever spent," he says. "It opened my eyes. It gave me knowledge I didn't have before. I saw that a lot of people were doing the same thing. I found more and better ways of how to dig up information."

IRE had been started by a group of like-minded journalists who thought the hard-earned knowledge gathered separately through their long years of reporting experience should be shared. The organization, now numbering 1,500 members, holds an annual conference and regional meetings featuring reports on various kinds of investigative reporting: presents awards for outstanding investigative reporting; publishes the *IRE Journal* four times a year and maintains a library of 2,000 investigative stories by print and broadcast reporters at its headquarters at the University of Missouri School of Journalism.

The organization's best known activity also helped add to the investigative reporter legend. In 1976, after *Arizona Republic* reporter Don Bolles was killed while looking into political corruption and organized crime in that state, an IRE team of volunteers from 27 newspapers and broadcast stations around the country went to Arizona to finish Bolles' work. The 23-part series of articles that resulted from the efforts of the Arizona Project won a special award from SPJ,SDX and some notoriety for IRE.

Uhrhammer became a member of the Arizona Project at the convention.

"At the time of the first meeting, Don Bolles, a charter member, had been dead two weeks," recalls Uhrhammer. "A resolution was passed at that first meeting to look into the feasibility of sending a task force into Arizona to complete his work and to show you can't kill a story by killing a reporter."

Uhrhammer went for three weeks, but wound up staying for three months. He worked on reporting the land fraud, political corruption and Arizona justice portions of the final articles and did some of the writing.

The Arizona Project was criticized by editors at some large newspapers as superficial, sensational and a new form of what they called "vigilante journalism."

A number of people mentioned in the articles filed libel suits ranging from $500,000 to $150 million, some of them still unsettled. "We're OK on the lawsuits," says Uhrhammer. "We've got documentation to back up everything."

Supporters point to a number of benefits coming from the articles, however: increased cooperation among law enforcement agencies because of the attention focused on crime in Arizona, higher budgets for law enforcement in the state, and the fact that they served as good background material for later investigations and indictments.

"It will never happen again," says Uhrhammer of the project, on whose behalf he had to appear in court as IRE president. "It was a gallant effort, a grassroots organization of reporters and an infant organization with the guts to try to pull if off. IRE pulled it off."

Guidelines for investigative reporting

Jerry Uhrhammer has his own set of rules for investigative reporting:

• *Read the applicable law or regulation.* "You need to know what the requirements of the law are and how they apply to whatever situation you're looking at."

• *Be objective and clinical.* "Some reporters go in with a sense of outrage. All of us have a sense of outrage when we start investigating something like the Bolles story, but you've got to be very clinical and separate emotion from . . . objective fact."

• *Look in terms of systems.* "Collect as much information as you can. Work on the paper trail, what exists on paper. Build and follow up on this. Write down on paper or in a VDT everything that happened in the order that it happened because many times a cause and effect relationship will become apparent. When you put widely separated incidents together, you see that one thing caused another to happen. This gives you an idea of who to talk to next and the questions to ask."

• *Ask, "is this a gettable story?"* "Do your sniff test. Some stories are not possible to get. Records are totally private and, short of burglary, there is simply no way to get a story if the people involved don't want you to have it, unless you can get someone inside. You must ascertain all of this early on."

• *Do not commit a burglary.* "Reporters should never break a law to get a story, it can come back to haunt them. If you end up in court— a judicial court or the court of public opinion—and it can be shown you broke the law to get it, this can destroy your work and your credibility. As investigative reporters, we spend most of the time delving into the violations of others. It's hypocritical if we violate laws to get that information."

• *Keep your nose clean.* "Avoid doing illegal or unethical things that, if somebody found out, could be used against you as blackmail to drop or change a story; I know, it has been tried with me. I don't worry. I try to keep my nose clean. You can't worry about threats to yourself and your family. I'm not concerned with my physical safety. I'm more concerned with being set up—drugs planted, etc. It behooves us as reporters to travel a straight path. You never know when someone will try to use something against you."

• *Prepare carefully for interviews.* "You've got to have background in order to follow the paper trail and know what to ask them" he says. "The paper trail alone is not enough. After you've built a skeleton of documents, you add the flesh with the interviews. You go to your sources and say, 'Here's what we have found. Is it true or not true?'

• *Verify everything.* "You've got to check out and verify source material thoroughly. Sometimes this is not possible. At other times you can check part of it. Before you go with something, give the other side the chance to deny or comment. Prevention is much better than coming back later and thinking, 'I should have done this.' "

• *Keep all documents in some orderly fashion.* Uhrhammer uses looseleaf notebooks to keep the material he collects on a story. He indexes everything by subject so he can find it easily. If the material is too bulky to fit in a notebook, he puts it in legal size accordian files.

• *A word about tape recorders.* "I use a tape recorder a great deal. It gives you a record, a way to backstop a quote. If you're just taking notes, you sometimes miss things. A tape gives you a better record. If you tape telephone calls, check out the state law. In Oregon, it is legal to do so without telling the other party. In some other states it is against the law to tape a telephone call without informing the other party. I also take extensive notes. It is terrible to be without your notes when the tape recorder doesn't work. You can fill in your notes by going over the tape. There's nothing like having the tapes."

Editing

Reading some of their stories each day for 38 months was a little like catching the vulnerable beauty queen without her makeup on. While many produced near-impeccable copy, just as many wrote prose that even a doting mother could learn to hate. The likes of so many misspelled words, dangling participles, split infinitives, misplaced modifiers, ludicrous analogies and time-worn phrases ('a heartbeat away,' etc.) had never passed before such young eyes in so much volume, not even in English composition classes.

Nancy Claire Campbell

Rewrite, the ability to take a mass of material from many reporters in the field over the telephone and turn it into a polished story, may be headed for extinction on all but a few big city newspapers. The job requires skills in writing and editing beyond those possessed by many reporters. It also demands speed and a surety in language, spelling, and style. A March 1974 story about how one of the best rewritemen in the country does his job reveals a great deal about an unknown and unsung position.

THE JOB IS REWRITE

Paul Galloway

THIS ONE CAME, as all big, breaking stories do, without a trumpet fanfare, and, like many of them, nerve-clenchingly close to deadline.

It was a slow Friday about an hour before copy was due for the first edition when the black telephone that is a direct line to the City News Bureau rang at City Desk. Its ringing generally means a story of some importance. Such was the case on that Friday afternoon of December 8, 1972.

"Bulletin," the voice on the phone said. "There's a plane down on the Southwest Side near Midway. It's a big airlines jet, a lot of people on board."

Leighton McLaughlin, the first assistant city editor, put down the phone, turned and began turning the activity from the routine to the extraordinary. It was not at all hard. As word of the crash rippled through the newsroom, the effect was instantaneous. It was as if a common adrenalin pump which fed the bloodstreams of the reporters had been switched on.

Newspaper people like big stories and they like to be tested at deadline. That accounts for the exhilaration that is part anxiety and part elation and always comes during a big one, although the elation is hidden under solemn expressions and businesslike chaos.

McLaughlin and City Editor Jim Peneff began pulling reporters from their original assignments and putting them on the Midway crash. Wire copy started coming in, and the phone headsets started going on. Deadline was then an hour away at 3:30 p.m., there was a replate at 6 p.m. and the major edition deadline at 9 p.m.

It was a big story, all right. Forty-five persons, including a congressman, a network television newswoman and Mrs. E. Howard Hunt, died in the crash, which leveled homes in a residential neighborhood. Seventeen reporters would work on the story. There would be eight sidebars. And the main story? Peneff and McLaughlin knew who would write the main story. It would be Hugh Hough.

Hugh Hough is the first violinist on the Chicago *Sun-Times* rewrite bank. He is a hell of a rewriteman. "He's the guy we go to in the clutch," says Peneff.

One reporter who was in the newsroom on his day off and who probably has seen "Deadline U.S.A." three or four times too many said he got tears in his eyes as he watched Hough (pronounced like "tough") take the calls from reporters on the scene, take the slips of wire copy, take the notes from reporters in the newsroom and then pound out 10 clean takes for the first edition. As the deadline passed, Hough kept on, updating the lead and adding new information for the next edition, and then the next.

It was something newspaper people appreciate, and they are about the only ones who *can* appreciate what a rewriteman does. Outside the newsroom, a rewriteman is as anonymous as an offensive lineman. He doesn't get Pulitzer Prizes, he doesn't get reader recognition, mainly he just gets the paper out.

Or at least did. The rewriteman is fading away. There is still a need for him, mostly on afternoon dailies and at the wire services, but The QUILL, in a quite random but unquestionably revealing survey, discovered that a number of papers, mostly morning ones, don't even claim to have such a person.

"Some newspapers are reluctant to admit having someone in that position. They think there's a stigma about rewrite," says Ralph Otwell, managing editor of the *Sun-Times*. "It's part of the personal journalism cult, I suppose. Some reporters don't want people to know they don't write their stories themselves. But having someone on rewrite, particularly on a breaking story, is unavoidable."

There was a time when the distinction between reporter and rewriteman was as sharply drawn as the roles of solicitor and barrister in the British legal system. A reporter reported and a rewriteman (and it was solely a man) wrote what the reporter reported.

That has gradually changed. "When I joined the *Sun-Times* in 1962," says Joe Reilly, an assistant city editor, "there was only one beat reporter who wrote his own stories. We used rewrite even when some reporters were capable of writing their own pieces. Not so much now."

"Rewrite can be overdone," says Otwell. "One way it was abused was to deny the younger people a chance to write."

But there are those like McLaughlin who believe rewrite is the best job on a paper and who feel it could be used more instead of less. "There is a lot of variety," he says. "You can go from a garden walk to an ax murder in one eight-hour shift. It gives you an opportunity to do a story on which you don't have to do all the legwork and you can spend more time writing for a living than reporting, which was a predilection of mine. It's also a hell of a lot of fun.

"You also get a more evenly written paper. It's another editing process for the reporter's story to go through. A reporter gives you as much as he's got, but the rewriteman can filter out the nonessential. And usually the rewriteman can write better than reporters."

There is something else. "The rewriteman is a way to train young reporters," says Peneff, "by telling them the questions to ask and the holes to fill in a story."

Roger Simon, a 25-year-old reporter who would not acknowledge a need for training even if a razor-sharp pica pole were held to his throat, will still concede that he picked up somethng from Hugh Hough when he called in one afternoon to report that Johnny Lindquist had died.

Johnny Lindquist was a 7-year-old who was in a coma for five weeks from a beating he received after he was returned from a foster home to his natural parents. Johnny's father was charged with beating Johnny because Johnny wet the bed, and the family had a past record of child abuse.

It was a tragic story that received prominent play for five weeks, touching readers and exhausting rewritemen, many of whom gave up trying to avoid phrases like "struggle for life" and "battle for life." Words like "valiant" popped up.

"It frankly was a relief in some ways when Johnny died," Simon says. "I called it in to Hough, and he did his typically great job. Other writers were writing tremendously overblown leads. One had a lead that's used when Presidents die—'Johnny Lindquist is dead.' But Hough wrote the perfect story without one cliche or purple phrase."

It began: "The troubled life of 7-year-old Johnny Lindquist ended peacefully Thursday in St. Anne Hospital."

The cliche, to the good rewriteman, is at least the eighth deadly sin. Most probably rank it higher and each time one is avoided, there is pride. For Hough, there is one word in particular that rankles.

While ranking hundreds of stories dealing with investigations over the last 15 years or so, he has not once used the word "probe" as a noun. It is, he says, a purely personal prejudice based on an aversion to headlinese. This prejudice, he admits, has required a heavy reliance on plain old "investigation," and, for a change of pace, "inquiry."

A number of newspapers have a Hugh Hough or perhaps a tradition of Hugh Houghs. At the *Sun-Times,* they still talk about Marvin Quinn, Bentley Stegner and Ray Brennan.

Stegner, who died in 1968, had a facility for distilling, which is the mark of a good rewriteman. "He was able to boil any complex story to two graphs and get everything important into them," sayd Otwell. "Stegner could listen to a police reporter for two hours and then produce a two-graph story that told it all. You would see him sitting there staring at his typewriter for three minutes, organizing. Then out would come the two graphs."

Marv Quinn was the quintessential rewriteman, big and soft-hearted with a fierce temper and a rare writing talent. He raised canaries, collected buffalo nickels, befriended kids, taught himself about the stock market during lulls on nightside and eventually made some money with his investments. Marvin Quinn suffered a cerebral hemorrhage at his typewriter one February day in 1964 and died 13 days later at age 54.

Quinn was identified in his obituary as "a *Sun-Times* rewriteman," a description that might not be used today. Today, a rewriteman is likely to be referred as "writer" or "news writer" or some other euphemistic title, at least in some places.

Ray Brennan wrote a tribute to Quinn in an office newsletter just after the rewriteman died. He said Quinn would throw into the wastebasket the start of a story that another writer might paste into a scrapbook. "There are few readers who would recognize his name—and for good reason," Brennan wrote. "He was no by-line hog. He insisted that the reporters get the billing rather than himself."

If rewrite has more anonymity and less glamour than by-lined reporting, it also has its compensations. There is the peer esteem, which means a lot. And a rewriteman is paid more than most reporters. That means a lot, too.

Ray Brennan, who died in 1972, was a rewriteman, but he was also a reporter who could investigate-muckrake-expose with the best. He specialized in organized crime and political corruption, two not insignificant or unrelated subject areas in Chicago, but he could just as deftly profile a Fidel Castro or an Elvis Presley and did.

Hough and his fellow rewritemen at the *Sun-Times* are like Brennan in their ability to both report and rewrite. Newspapers have a need for such flexibility.

"People are not hired in a strict category anymore," says *Sun-Times* Editor James Hoge. "In that way, things have changed. There used to be any number of reporters who didn't know one end of a pencil from another, but that's not true anymore. The premium is on those who can do several things well. A reporter is expected to write well in addition to reporting. But in a multi-edition, hard-news-oriented newspaper a person like Hugh Hough is absolutely essential."

Maybe it's the term that confuses some and causes others to avoid using "rewriteman." The word simply doesn't mean anything to the layman. Most assume that the rewriteman rewrites, whatever that might be. Even the newsroom's unabridged Webster's fails to define what a rewriteman does.

But just listen to City Editor Peneff talk about what makes Hugh Hough a good rewriteman, a good newspaperman:

Has superb news judgment. Versatility. Can write a light reader, handle a legally delicate piece or clarify a terribly complicated story, quickly and on deadline. Cool. Copy needs virtually no editing. Totally accurate. Physical strength. Got to be able to work 15 hours at a stretch. Have to be in damned good condition. It's a nerve-wracking job.

And, Peneff adds, Hugh Hough volunteers for obits, a task so utterly devoid of appeal with even cub reporters that it can inspire wailing and gnashing of Dixon Flamingo No. 303 point pencils.

Who is Hugh Hough and what is he really like? He was born 50 years ago this April in Sandwich, Illinois, a farming community 60 miles west of Chicago which has grown in the last half century from 2,612 to 4,500 souls. There is a newspaperman in his family tree—a great-great-grandfather who started the first newspaper in DeKalb County—but it was a high school English teacher who recognized his talent for writing and encouraged him in it.

He was a gunner in a B-24 crew that flew 32 missions in Italy and Germany in World War II, developing an iron butt that has served him well on the rewrite bank. He went to the University of Illinois on the GI Bill, majoring in journalism and becoming editor of the *Daily Illini* in his senior year. He started as a $55-a-week sports editor of the Dixon (Ill.) *Evening Telegraph* in 1951. A year and a half later, he applied for a place on the copy desk of the *Sun-Times.* He was asked to spell "accommodate," blew it by omitting a "c" but got the job anyway, soon being made a general assignment reporter.

He has covered the funerals of Dwight Eisenhower and Martin Luther King and recently collaborated with Art Petacque on the Valerie Percy murder case. He and Petacque have painted a convict into a corner with irrefutable circumstantial evidence in the 1966 crime. The murder is, in effect, solved.

Petacque, a reporter who doesn't write but can and does fill a newspaper with stories, handling several simultaneously, has worked with Hough for years. They make a formidable battery, and their relationship is a perfect mesh.

One of the first really big ones Hough handled on rewrite was the Our Lady of the Angels School fire of December 1, 1958. Eighty-seven children and three nuns died. Hough sat at his desk for 10 hours, writing stories and subbing each for four editions.

"I suppose it is a cliche," Hough says, uncharacteristically risking one, "but deadline writing is clearer and better reading than the stuff you agonize over. You fall back on the simple declarative sentence, which in the final analysis is the best there is."

That, incidentally, is a long conversation for Hugh Hough. He does not say much. When he does, he is soft-spoken. He does not lose his temper and he is unflappable. There is such an aura of calm about Hough, people within a 10-foot radius tend to feel drowsy. He may beat his wife, Ellen, and scream at his four children, but it's doubtful.

Does he have any rules? "The obvious, common sense one of not falling into traps. Stay on the conservative side when you're not sure of the facts."

Is the rewrite changing? "We're getting more good young reporters and old reporters, too, who can write their own stories well. Still, on a breaking story. . . ."

Does he mind the public obscurity (even though he received the paper's top award in 1969)? "No, I like it when a reporter tells me he thought I did a good job with his story."

And the strong constitution? Hough says he's lucky not to have missed a single day's work since 1954. "I got the flu once, but it was Thanksgiving Day."

Recently, Hough got some recognition. He and Petacque were asked to appear on a television talk show to discuss their investigation of the murder of Senator Percy's daughter. Hough was asked if he had been working on the Percy case since it happened.

"No, not exclusively," Hough replied. "I'm a rewriteman."

The television host didn't respond. It was obvious the guy didn't know what the hell a rewriteman was.

The day in the life of a newspaper copy editor is a day in the life of a nearly anonymous person. No glory awaits the person who spends the day looking for spelling errors, split infinitives, and style book violations. Reporters consider any stint on the desk as a kind of journalistic Siberia. Nancy Claire Campbell, who worked as a copy editor for the *Birmingham* (Alabama) *News* before becoming a reporter, recalls the trials and tribulations of time on the desk in this May 1977 article.

STORY OF A COPY EDITOR: THE PRISONER OF ZENDA SAYS THANKS

Nancy Claire Campbell

For an ambitious 22-year-old, the prospect of ending professional life in the newsroom "graveyard" was grim, indeed. A writing career scarcely begun surely was doomed, I thought, if I accepted a position on a large metropolitan daily as copy editor. After all, desk jobs aren't exactly coveted by young j-school grads desperately wanting to set the world ablaze with their imagined writing and reportorial skills.

It's an old story, really. But this one has a happy ending I didn't believe possible at a time when the cruel cliche, repeated too often by those who presume to know everything about the news business, dominated my thoughts: "Those who can, write; and those who can't, read copy."

With that bitter refrain stinging my pride, I actually was arrogant enough to turn down the managing editor's initial offer with the pretense that the pay was too low. Even my menial tasks at less pay as public relations writer for a nearby university seemed preferable to correcting misspelled words for the rest of my life. If my p.r. responsibilities weren't exciting (mostly, I wrote up the awarding of federal grants), at least those words were mine. And besides, weren't all copy editors just a bunch of graying old men who sat around puffing their pipes all day? No death wish for me, thank you. Only writing would do.

In retrospect, such egotism is unfathomable. Credit is due a persistent m.e., bent on hiring a young woman, who rebounded with the higher salary offer that eventually lured me to the job that taught me more about good writing than a beat or any well-meaning city editor serving as mentor can offer a novice reporter.

Upon leaving the copy desk three years later, my new colleagues on city side of the newsroom presented me with the "Prisoner of Zenda Award" during an awards spoof, for "surviving the anonymity of the copy desk." They reasoned that my "rise to prominence" as new writer on the staff warranted so prestigious an honor.

While laughing good-naturedly, I couldn't help recalling the sound news judgment I'd gained and the high regard for our language I'd acquired at the copy desk—an experience they all missed. My education was the study of their literary strengths and weaknesses.

Reading some of their stories each day for 38 months was a little like catching the vulnerable beauty queen without her makeup on. While many produced near-impeccable copy, just as many wrote prose that even a doting mother could learn to hate. The likes of so many misspelled words, dangling participles, split infinitives, misplaced modifiers, ludicrous analogies and time-worn phrases ("a heartbeat away," etc.) had never passed before such young eyes in so much volume, not even in English composition classes.

The copy desk still guffaws over one author's writing "the water lapped wetly against the rock." And did you know than an interstate highway system resembles "a mass of arteries pulsating to the throbbing heart of the city?"

The point in all of this is not to criticize unduly. To err is human, as they say; so skilled copy editors graciously accept their duties as newsroom janitors, as it were. Besides, there is an important lesson in this. About the time smug editors start feeling a little superior to their sometimes less articulate, sometimes theatrical friends behind typewriters, they make blunders that keep one's face red for days.

First lesson in careful editing: Never fall into the pit labeled Double Meaning, particularly if the words will cause confusion or embarrassment. The pitfall is the most treacherous in headline writing because stories often aren't read.

I thought the head, "Coed has 10-pound rabbit," was dull. But so was the tepid story about the university student who kept a pet rabbit in her dormitory room. The next day, a tear sheet appeared on the bulletin board and some wiseacre had scribbled: "Mother and bunny rabbit are doing well." I like to blame that one on inexperience.

Thank goodness, I didn't write the head (in 60-point type no less) that made pornographic history of sorts. At the height of Watergate when President Nixon was being pressured to resign, a truly distinguished senior editor carelessly headlined the Associated Press story: "Nixon says he'll stick it out." Playboy magazine picked it up and friends I hadn't heard from in months called to congratulate my ultra-conservative paper on the dubious distinction of "outdoing itself." "Just the pickup we need in time of national crisis," one caller quipped. Maybe so, but it was purely unintentional.

Remember when then energy czar William Simon made the papers every day during the 1974 fuel crisis? Our banner head beginning "Simon says" lent a certain silliness to a serious matter, instantly conjuring up memories of "May I."

Many subscribers think their paper is the gospel, so no one knows better than the copy editor that words must be used precisely. A poor choice of words in headline or text can be disastrous for the simple reason that they *are* in print. The printed word is impressive, and it carries considerably more weight than the spoken word. Public speakers and broadcast journalists might get away with poor sentence construction or an occasional hackneyed expression that is soon forgotten. They don't even have to spell correctly. But there's no salvation for the printed word. It is there for all the world to read, reread and criticize. There's no glossing over what's been said. Even a retraction won't undo 100 percent of the damage, because everyone who read the offensive piece might not have seen the correction.

Life in the Graveyard

Since editing is a constant adventure in writing, there should be no shocking revelations in the profession. However, my vulnerability to shock was limitless. For weeks I'd noticed that one reporter was misspelling the same words repeatedly. Since I considered it part of my job to point out such errors, I asked him without sarcasm why he didn't use the dictionary more often. "I never learned how," he answered with a sigh. Disarmed, I repeated the question to make sure I understood him. It turned out that a man possessing a master's degree in journalism from the state university really couldn't use the basic tool of his trade. For years, he relied on others who spelled for him.

Perhaps weak writers are overprotected by good copy editors. Slovenliness is easy to rationalize by reporters who figure that errors won't escape desk scrutiny. But copy editors have no refuge. They are positively nude in their exposure since errors that do pass cease to be the reporters'. A boiling m.e. demanding to know "Who wrote this head?" or "Who handled this story?" isn't uncommon, and the reporter involved might never know there was an incident.

Traditionally, the copy desk has been considered a graveyard for worn-out reporters who can't hack deadline pressures anymore. If that's true, then I reversed the process by becoming a reporter reincarnate. But I don't think the cemetery that journalism professors and successful writers warned me against necessarily exists. It's true that some editors are has-been hot-shot reporters, but many more are storehouses of information who often rate among a paper's best writers.

One of my co-workers was the rewrite man on the Pulitzer Prize-winning team at a western newspaper that covered the collision of two planes over Grand Canyon in 1956. He continued to write his weekly humor column, another award-winner, for fun at my paper until his death last year.

Unencumbered by the confines of a beat, editors on universal desks are barraged with ever-changing situations in city, state, national and international news. The effective copy editor doesn't buckle under the strain of having to know a little or a lot about virtually everything.

When one story about a rabble-rousing, whisky-guzzling public figure called for an accompanying photograph, and the picture of a dignified former First Lady inadvertently was substituted, a quick-witted copy editor came to the rescue. Although the former governor's wife had been a private citizen for years, the man vaguely remembered her. He had no idea what the woman in the story looked like, so he checked her out. Whew, a close one!

It was frightening enough for one so young among 12 men a generation or two older that editors are expected to be champion spellers, grammarians and must know press law. But they also should be historians, sociologists, geographers and, yes, even diplomats.

Spare the Writer's Message

How far should an editor go too improve a poorly written piece? My rule is to rewrite as little as possible but as much as necessary in the limited time available without destroying the author's original message. If the story is so garbled that the message isn't clear and the reporter isn't around for consultation, then lots of luck. Maybe a little educated guesswork will help. Maybe.

Always remember the reporter's ubiquitous ego. One of the reasons he chose journalism in the first place was because he loves to see his name in print, so the editor should try to imagine himself in the reporter's position. It won't do to lay him too low with the blue pencil. He probably won't notice that the editor corrected his erroneous use of the subjunctive for the fortieth time, but the slashing of a precious sentence or paragraph seldom eludes him.

Youth is an asset in diplomacy. I casually could suggest improvements to writers without making them uncomfortable. I wasn't the ominously authoritative figure other editors presented. In pointing out an error, I might play the tease and say, "My third-grade text said never do this." If the reporter replied he didn't remember that rule, I'd say, "I know." Usually, we'd both laugh. I couldn't afford getting too cocky since writers also taught me a lesson or two each day.

Obviously, editing isn't glamorous. Copy readers don't win prizes or rub elbows with famous personalities. The work is monotonous, tedious, often boring, and there's absolutely no praise or recognition associated with it. Copy editors don't get bylines. If the president comes to town in an election year, the copy editor won't see him because he's back at the office awaiting the story. And at the end of the day, when most reporters on afternoon papers have gone home, at least one copy editor is in the composing room making up the market-finals edition that hits newsstands when businessmen and women get off about 5 p.m.

Terms like pica, em, velox, font, true count and double truck often are enigmas to reporters concerned only with writing the news. Processing of the news demands that editors be mechanics who can make words fill the space in a way that's typographically acceptable, consistent with a paper's style, journalistically correct, artistic (to a degree) and marketable. It isn't unusual that editors must write cutlines for photographs they may never have seen. And then there's the scanner. Reporters at papers using the computerized system of setting type must know a few basic rules, but the editor must understand the process from A to Z if it's to work efficiently. A story's text carelessly set in 48-point type makes amusing bulletin board material, but scanner operators fail to see the humor.

Having Earned Self-Confidence

Anyone seeking newspaper employment who's been turned off to editing by this account probably didn't have the backbone for it anyway. But a young person willing to learn writing skills in a high-pressure situation will be rewarded immeasurably on the desk.

I didn't think I was being rewarded while holding my nose to all those 4:30 a.m. and Saturday-night shifts, but the self-confidence in writing I earned is worth more to me now than all those pats on the back I never received.

My old copy desk chief's advice was the best. "Hang tough," he liked to say. The "graveyard" doesn't have to be the end of the world. I resumed writing at age 26, and it wasn't too late.

Next to a good dictionary, the stylebook is an important part of every copy editor's (and reporter's) day. Some news organizations develop their own style and style books; many use the style books of Associated Press and United Press International. In 1977, both wire services published new style books. Eileen Alt Powell, then an AP reporter/editor in New York and now on the staff of the *Wall Street Journal,* worked on the AP book and wrote about the changes in the July-August 1977 issue of *The Quill.* Fledgling reporters should come away from this article with an appreciation of how seriously news organizations take style.

MEDIA (IS) (ARE) GETTING NEW 'BIBLE': STYLEBOOK PUBLICATION UNDER WAY (2 WORDS)

Eileen Alt Powell

It was two o'clock on a Sunday morning, a quiet time in the world and the news business. So why had editor Howard Angione just walked in the Associated Press office?

"What's the matter, Howard? Can't sleep?" teased one member of the overnight crew.

While many would spurn the midnight-to-dawn shift, for Angione it proved ideal. It was then he could work in peace at a video display terminal that technicians had specially rigged for his part in the joint AP-UPI effort to develop a new, common stylebook.

Print-outs made from Angione's computer terminal were carried by messenger each afternoon to United Press International 12 blocks away. There UPI editor Bobby Ray Miller read them, wrote comments and inserts, and returned the material by courier to the AP. And the cycle began again—an uncommon cycle in the traditional rivalry of two large news organizations, and only part of what turned out to be a two-year effort to meet on some mutually agreeable, verbal ground.

Publication of the long-awaited revised AP and UPI stylebooks began in late June (1977). Distribution is scheduled to begin sometime this month. Although different in format and sometimes in form, both books are based on the guidelines agreed to by Angione and Miller.

But saying that, and just that, makes such a project appear oh so easy. It wasn't.

This should come as no surprise to those who have been anticipating the arrival of a new stylebook. There were reports in 1976 that we would be seeing one shortly after the first of the year. And the AP Log of Jan. 10, 1977, said: "Publication of the book is expected in March."

But there were too many unexpected diversions along the way. Like the frequent telephone calls inquiring of the editors how the news services intended to handle "Ms." Like the occasional arguments over entries between Angione and Miller, sometimes requiring arbitration by their bosses.

Arguments between the two were inevitable. Each had to justify an entry he wrote to the other. On loan from the national desks of their respective news services, Angione and Miller dug in from the start and concentrated their efforts on what to them was a serious assignment. And it's that attitude that may help explain why the process took so long. The AP and UPI knew that this revision would be the journalist's bible for years to come. They wanted it to be right.

The news services first worked to develop a common style in the late 1950s. Uniformity had been sought by newspapers whose copy desks often were forced to grapple with different spellings, punctuation and abbreviations in stories on the same topic from the two wires.

These early books—which became the reference works for hundreds of college journalism courses, the "official" stylebook of many newspapers and the handbook for all AP and UPI staffers—were updated jointly in the late 1960s.

But new needs and new questions arose. Couldn't rules such as "use figures in all man or animal ages; spell under 10 for inanimates" be simplified? Reporters and editors sought guidance on "new" words: Is "astronaut" capitalized when used as a title? Is "gay" a noun when applied to the homosexual movement? Is "kilohertz" a replacement for "kilocycle"?

The time had come for another meeting of the wires. Thousands of hours of research and review by staff members, newspaper editors and technical specialists went into this latest effort. Out of it came nearly 5,000 entries. A few disagreements between the two wire services never were resolved—whether "media" should be used as a plural or singular noun, for example, or whether one should write the Prince of Wales the prince of Wales. But the books to be distributed this month and next show a consistency and depth much improved over previous editions.

Each stylebook has grown from 52 pages. AP's has 276 pages; UPI's is 195 pages long.

In both books, the old topical arrangement of chapters—capitalization, abbreviation, spelling, etc.—has given way to an alphabetical listing of rules and the words included for style, spelling or usage purposes. Many entries in both manuals are cross-referenced.

Also new are explanatory entries on topics such as metric conversions, weather terminology, the tenets of major religions, and the subdivisions within nations or alliances.

"As work progressed, we became convinced that while style would remain the chief purpose, there were many factual references we should include to make things easier for busy editors. So we have a stylebook, but also a reference work," AP Executive Editor Louis D. Boccardi explains in the introduction of his stylebook.

One such reference entry covers earthquakes. It explains the differences between the Richter and Mercalli scales, lists the quakes noted for magnitude and damage and defines such terms as "temblor" and "epicenter."

The names of participating colleges appear under "Big Ten" conference.

Entries on corporations, unions and associations give the locations of headquarters.

"Inches" contains the equation for converting to centimeters; "centimeters" has the reverse.

Under the heading "weather terms" in the AP stylebook are definitions used by the National Weather Service for "blizzard," "flood," "gale," "hurricane" and "winter storm watch." The stylebook advises that a "blizzard requires winds of 35 mph or more and considerable falling and/or blowing snow with visibility near zero." Each weather term is listed alphabetically in the UPI book.

Charting a Path

Howard Angione, who worked on the AP stylebook from early 1975 until he departed for the New York Times in April of 1971, at times thought the task he and UPI counterpart Bobby Ray Miller had undertaken resembled the quest of Don Quixote. It was "an impossible dream," Angione said, to find style rules that pleased everyone, especially since even grammarians couldn't agree among themselves.

Miller was surprised at the research required on some topics. "A lot of things are a lot more difficult to find than you would think," he said. He recalled, for example, that one of his co-workers felt the terms "Third World" and "non-aligned" frequently were confused in news stories. "It took him a week and a half to come up with definitions that got the point across," Miller said. "And he is a student of foreign affairs."

The path was clear in some areas. What to include began, of course, with the study of the contents of the old AP and UPI stylebooks. Then came suggestions for updates and revisions from newspaper editors, solicited in newsletters, and from the news services' staff members.

The AP added some of its own path markers. Walter G. Cowan, editor of the States-Item in New Orleans, solicited and registered suggestions from AP members. There also was a list of 50 most common errors, compiled by a committee of the AP Managing Editors Association in 1974. (Among them: You "allude" to, or mention, a book. You "elude," or escape, a pursuer.) And a list of hundreds of commonly misspelled words (does "accommodate" come to mind?) that now-retired A-wire filer Jerry Yale had come across during his 35-year career.

It wasn't long before the editors encountered the first windmills on their quest—selecting a backup dictionary, deciding on courtesy titles for women and settling on a joint format for capitalization. And debate on any of these is not likely to be silenced by publication of the stylebooks.

Angione remembers "a number of nights that first year when I went home from work and read dictionaries." The old stylebook had drawn heavily from Webster's Second International, the tome from the G. & C. Merriam Co. that sits on a centrally located stand in many newsrooms.

Webster's Third International had been published, and it was a likely candidate as backup for the new stylebook. Wordsmith's however, were concerned that the new, big dictionary did not pay sufficient attention to usage: "teener" was the equal of "teen-ager," with no guidance on which was more appropriate for formal use, which for colloquial.

Several alternative books were reviewed and rejected.

The news services finally selected Webster's New World Dictionary of the American Language, Second College Edition, published by the William Collins-World Publishing Co. Entries are clean, usage is emphasized and a full-time staff at Collins-World continually studies current publications and updates citations. Webster's Third International remained "in" as the source for information not found in the stylebook or Webster's New World. Among the other backup sources are the Columbia Lippincott Gazetteer of the World, Jan's All the World's Aircraft, Lloyd's Register of Shipping and the Congressional Directory.

Angione said he had been impressed with the philosophy expressed by Editor-in-Chief David B. Guralnik in the introduction to Webster's New World and that many stylebook entries reflected that philosophy. "The issue is not one of 'permissiveness' versus 'authoritarianism,' " Guralnik wrote. "No lexicographer, at least in this country, has been given a mandate either to permit or to disallow any usage. He has, however, assumed the responsibility of informing the public of the state of the language as of the time during which his dictionary was compiled."

The toughest "state of the language" question the stylebook editors encountered concerned "Mrs.," "Miss" and "Ms." Both services put the issue to their members. Angione and Boccardi brought the subject up at as many AP gatherings as they could. Ten options were developed and sent to editors for consideration. Executives met with groups of newswomen who advocated abandonment of all courtesy titles.

As people outside the profession became aware of the discussions, letters began to come in:

"Drop all the titles!"

"Don't you dare!"

"Treat women's names the same as men's."

"I'm a Mrs. and I want to be called a Mrs."

All these points of view (and perhaps a few more) found favor somewhere among newspaper members. But this consensus soon became clear to the stylebook editors: Since usage varies widely and since the traditional forms remain the norm in many places, the AP and UPI should put the titles "Miss," "Mrs." and "Ms." in the copy and members can take them out if that suits local fashion.

"Mr." is not to be used in any reference unless it is combined with "Mrs." ("Mr. and Mrs. John Smith, Mr. and Mrs. Smith").

A Place for Last Names Only

But now to the sports pages—and a continuing controversy, for it is on the sports wires where the stylebook editors decided to drop the courtesy titles for women. Some outside observers are puzzled about this. Others are angry. Still others are amused. They all want to know why the apparent inconsistent treatment of women's names. After all, news and sports both are part of each edition of a family newspaper. Isn't this only confusing the issue? the critics ask.

Dropping the courtesy titles for women in sports stories only follows a precedent set for men, explained AP Vice President Louis Boccardi. "The dropping of 'Mr.' on the sports wires years ago had to do with the more informal circumstances and tone on the sports pages. It [the move this time to drop the use of "Mrs," "Miss" and "Ms."] seemed like an appropriate change to make and was consistent with all the changes we made. Whether this will lead to the last-naming of women on news pages remains to be seen. As this is reviewed, we will be guided by what AP members want to use in their papers."

The new joint stylebook also contains entries on sexism in news writing, an outgrowth of some of the discussions about courtesy titles. The entry on "women" begins: "Women should receive the same treatment as men in all areas of coverage." The corresponding "man, mankind" entry advises that "humanity," "a person" or "an individual" are good substitutes in stories involving both men and women.

But there was no solution except to go their separate ways on some of the traditional disputes between AP and UPI. In the old stylebook, each news service developed its own procedures, AP opting, in some cases, for capital letters, UPI choosing lower case.

In this stylebook revision, again Angione and Miller selected, then rejected, a half-dozen schemes. And it wasn't until October, when the stylebook editors sat down with AP and UPI news executives that decisions were made which supposedly took into account the best of both wires.

But don't tell that to the Prince of Wales. The one area of capitalization where AP and UPI part ways is in formal titles standing alone or following the persons' names and set off by commas. The Prince of Wales, as far as the AP is concerned, is a title of British nobility that substitutes for a name. For UPI, the prince of Wales will suffice. So will the queen of England. Both news services require capitalization if a formal title precedes a name.

UPI is also less rigid when it comes to the use of the dictionary. Slang or colloquial expressions, according to Bobby Ray Miller, will be permitted in UPI copy. "Any word listed in the dictionary may be used for any of the definitions listed as long as the UPI stylebook does not specifically restrict its use or unless the dictionary labels the use substandard," Miller explained. By contrast, the AP book advises: "If the dictionary cautions that a particular usage is objected to by some linguists or is not accepted widely, be wary of the usage unless there is a reason in the context."

UPI, then, will allow "media" to be followed by a singular verb in a usage such as: "The media is opposed to prior restraint." The AP requires a plural verb with "media" at all times. UPI also will allow "Who do you wish to see?". The AP requires "whom."

Sorting It Out

The mechanics of developing the nearly 5,000 entries in the AP-UPI stylebook and putting them in book form also required teamwork (and paperwork, as three file cabinets at the AP bear witness to).

Angione and Miller met weekly to exchange the half-sheets of paper on which each had written entries. The information was checked and double-checked against the dictionaries, the gazetteer, federal documents, almanacs and trade association publications.

In May 1977, Angione typed the material from the half-sheets into the AP computer. By September, Angione and Miller had run three "private" printings from the computer and followed each with a major rewrite.

The stylebook got its most thorough review in December. One hundred copies of the manual were made in the AP print shop and distributed for comment to AP and UPI executives and editors, bureau chiefs and news editors, university professors with expertise in style, newspaper editors and members of the APME Writing and Editing Committee.

"They caught a few mistakes," Angione said. "Hyphens were a problem. There were some others, like we had misread the dictionary on 'underway.' "

(The December draft had said "underway—one word, all uses." The final stylebooks read: "under way—two words in virtually all uses: The project is under way. The naval maneuvers are under way. One word only when used as an adjective before a noun in a nautical sense: an underway flotilla.")

Changes have been made that may require some adjustment: "Employee" now ends with two e's; "percent" is one word; Canadian provinces are not to be abbreviated in datelines to avoid confusion over such abbreviations as "P.E.I."; "Tex." is out; "mph" has no periods; "president" (including reference to the president of the United States) and "pope" are lowercase when not preceding a name, in keeping with the general rule that titles are lowercase when standing alone; figures are used for all ages, betting odds, dates, dimensions, percentages, ratios, speeds and temperatures (except zero).

Other changes are more subtle: The "mailman" entry, for example, reads: "Letter carrier is preferable, because many women hold this job."

A few other changes are temporizations. Both stylebooks include dozens of metric entries and conversion formulas. UPI decided against providing guidelines on their use "because it was considered a policy question, and we didn't think our stylebook was the place for policy," Miller said. The AP decided to give this advice:

"Use metric figures when they are the primary form in which the source of a story has provided statistics. Follow the metric units with equivalents in the terms more widely known in the United States. . . .

"Provide metric equivalents for traditional forms if a metric unit has become widely known. As speedometers with kilometer markings become more prevalent, for example, a story about speed limits might list miles per hour and provide kilometers per hour in parentheses."

The experience of several newspapers indicates that the public and, in some cases, journalists are not ready for a total shift to metrics. The stylebooks are ready when they are.

Transsexual, Second Reference

Journalists who have to look things up for awhile can find consolation that even Angione did his share of hunting, occasionally to his chagrin. Recently, a General Desk editor called Angione with a question. He was editing a story on Rene Richards, a tennis player in the news after he underwent a sex-change operation and began competing as a woman.

"What," the editor asked Angione, "is the proper second-reference to a transsexual?"

Angione grabbed his stylebook draft and looked up "transsexual." Nothing. But he knew there should be something because he had written the entry himself.

"It took me 15 minutes to find it," Angione admitted later. "It was under 'sex changes.' It's now cross-referenced."

For three years, Richard L. Tobin, onetime executive editor of *Saturday Review* and now a journalism professor at Indiana University, has conducted a survey of newspaper and magazine editors about the use of language. The results indicate what worries the men and women who pass judgment on what goes into the pages of their pages—and what stays out. David Weaver, associate professor of journalism and director of the Bureau of Media Research at Indiana University, worked with Mr. Tobin on the first survey.

AT THIS POINT IN TIME—NEWSPAPER AND MAGAZINE EDITORS ON THE USE OF LANGUAGE: A SURVEY

Richard L. Tobin and David Weaver

Winstons may taste good like a cigarette should, but to the majority of copy chiefs on leading newspapers and magazines in the country, "like" as a conjunction is distasteful. To split an infinitive, e.g. to wrongly split an infinitive, is wrong, the copy masters say. And almost every deskman will tell you that fewer mistakes in editing copy are always more welcome than less mistakes.

These are some of the findings of a survey of copy chiefs on the use of language.

The survey, conducted at Indiana University, was an attempt to find out how journalists strike a balance between standard English and common usage.

The survey's respondents found most objectionable the indiscriminate use of "fewer" and "less." Ninety-seven out of the 100 copy editors queried would change the sentence, "There were less people in the auditorium last night . . ." to "There were fewer . . . " Eighty-eight percent of the editors would correct a split infinitive, and 67 percent of the editors would not have approved the copy for the Winston ad.

"Point in time"—a phrase that took hold after John Dean repeated it during the Watergate hearings—would have 95 percent of the editors reaching quickly for their blue pencils.

"Plus," at the beginning of a sentence, would be deleted by 80 percent. "Hopefully," in almost any context, would be changed by 73 percent.

Magazines are not newspapers, the responses made clear. The New Yorker and other leading magazines use the "Harvard comma" or "serial comma" before the conjunction in a word series. "It's not wrong," the New York Times editors said about the retention of that last comma, "it's simply not newspaper style." Other respondents from newspapers agreed.

Newspaper copy editors were hesitant to make other changes that magazine editors had no qualms about. When using a quotation by a newsmaker, only a few newspaper copy editors would correct the speaker's grammar, even when it came to the correct usage of the words listed here earlier and so staunchly defended by the copy editors: "like," "plus," "hopefully." Magazine editors, on the other hand, aren't as concerned with using direct quotes. By the time a piece of copy gets to a magazine editor, any number of quotes may have been laundered or paraphrased.

Several editors, especially those on large national magazines, pointed out that usage often depends on circumstance. "It depends how colloquial we want to be, whether it's in the title, blurb or text . . ." rather than a hard and fast policy for the whole of the magazine, said Jean Pascoe, senior editor at Woman's Day.

Time magazine correspondent Maria Luisa Cisneros said of her publication: "We can tell you that while we have great respect for proper English usage, and follow it at all times, we are inclined to be a bit more generous than some other publications—particularly magazines—in our use of words and phrases that haven't quite made it to Webster."

On newspapers, some editors suggested that sports pages have a somewhat wider latitude of language than the news pages. They went on to suggest that editorial pages are especially discriminating about the precise rules of grammar.

The demographics of the respondents did not seem to have too much bearing on the editing choices they said they would make. There was not much difference in the answers given by male and female editors, although the men did tend to be a bit more conservative in altering style over time. For example, the 24 women in the study were more likely to retain the "Harvard comma"— not the general practice of newspapers, but one which seems to be gaining recognition these days—than were the 76 men. Editors of publications with small circulations tended to be more reluctant to change habits of style than their counterparts on publications of larger circulations. Surprisingly, there were few differences in the editing decisions of those 57 editors who said they were journalism majors in college and those who said they were not.

A number of newspaper and magazine editors enumerated language devices they found bothersome:

Words that end in "ize" and "wise."

Use of the passive voice. One editor put it bluntly: "It's becoming harder and harder to find strong, stimple, active sentences!"

"Bureaucratese" and other "-eses" that make language more confusing and less precise.

"Different than" instead of "different from."

"In" words and phrases. Leonard Johnson of the Omaha World-Herald listed "gays" as particularly offending. He suspects that television commercials have much to do with what he calls the rise in "bastardized words."

Vulgarities offend many of America's top editors. Some write that four-letter words and locker-room expletives add nothing to most stories and can easily be avoided, even in quotations.

Vince Vanter, news editor of the Memphis Press-Scimitar, echoed the opinion of a number of respondents when he wrote of a strong resentment of the incursion of new words into acceptable print language: "All changes bother me. Language should not be fashionable. It should be steadfast."

On the other hand, the vast majority of those responding to the survey seemed aware that language does change constantly and that modern usage is forever driving out standard diction, often replacing it in time. If this were not the case we would still be using Shakespeare's "contumely" for scorn or contempt, "whilom" for once or formerly, "calumny" for slander, "penury" for want or destitution, "craven" for cowardly or afraid, and "thou" for you.

In October 1979, Tobin and Weaver sent questionnaires on English usage to editors of 50 randomly selected newspapers of circulations from 50,000 to 100,000, to 106 newspapers of circulations greater than 100,000 and to 50 leading magazines. The sample of magazines, while not a random one, was drawn up by Tobin. He selected the 50 magazines, which ranged in circulation from 25,000 to more than five million, for their high editorial standards.

By the end of 1979, the researchers received responses from 100 editors: 17 (34 percent) from the smaller circulation newspapers, 63 (59 percent) from the larger circulation newspapers and 20 (40 percent) from magazines.

Each questionnaire listed 10 words or phrases that seem to be gaining acceptance in American journalism. The 10 examples were taken from a newspaper or magazine published in the United States last year. The editors were asked if they would approve the listed usage or change it. Then they were asked to rate their opinions about the usage on a five-point scale from "strongly approve" to "strongly disapprove." The editors were encouraged to write about any other changing styles in language that they found particularly bothersome.

The questionnaire also asked each respondent for his or her years of experience in journalism, job title, age, sex, level of education and journalism training in college.

NEWSPAPER AND MAGAZINE EDITORS
ON LANGUAGE USAGE

Examples from current newspapers and magazines	Number of editors who would change usage (Total = 100)	Number of editors who "strongly disapprove" (Total = 100)
There were *less* people in the auditorium last night . . .	97	86
The Nixon committee believed it had enough evidence for a bill of impeachment at this point *in time.*	95	81
It should be finally settled during that period *of time.*	94	65
Union officials said they want *to* definitely *vote* on the contract tonight.	88	44
Flashlight batteries are *liable* to conk out if left for long in a drawer.	85	48
Hopefully, the White House will weather the attacks on the SALT treaty.	80	60

Examples from current newspapers and magazines	Number of editors who would change usage (Total = 100)	Number of editors who "strongly disapprove" (Total = 100)
The California Angels did best of all this winter. They purchased a shortstop, second baseman, and utility infielder. (Serial comma)	79	28
Plus, she isn't very bright.	73	44
It looks *like* the Dodgers have blown it for 1979.	67	31
The education commissioner expects to *contact* the teachers tomorrow morning.	27	3

THE LATEST WORD

Richard L. Tobin

The temperature of the average healthy human body is 98.6 and that is precisely the percentage of top newspaper and magazine editors in a recent survey who would not allow "irregardless" in copy when the writer meant "irrespective" or "regardless."

Equally strong is the American editor's hatred of "who" for "whom," and vice-versa in improper contexts. These two aversions lead the list of bête noires in the second nationwide usage survey conducted by the journalism school at Indiana University.

The survey indicates how journalists strike a balance between standard dictionary-approved English and common usage, which is forever trying to attain lingual respectability.

Almost 96 percent of those surveyed this year said they would change such phrases as "most unique," "quite unique" or "very unique," on grounds that "unique" cannot be modified.

Another item that horrifies copy desk people from coast to coast is the growing list of "governmentalisms," such as "to finalize," etc. This set off a comment from Susan B. Hohn, copy chief at Time magazine: "A trend that also fills us with alarm is the changing of nouns into verbs, to wit: 'Scripps-Howard is *officed* in Cincinnati' or 'Time Inc. is *headquartered* in New York City.' " Two other nouns that are sometimes put to work as verbs are "premiered" and "debuted." Irving Kolodin, music critic of Saturday Review, finds them anathema not only because they have been converted from one part of speech to another "but because they torture words from another language (French) into an English misappropriation."

Nearly every editor would change "alright" to "all right." And all but a few would change "different than" to "different from." Similarly, misuse of "that" and "which" irks 85 percent of U.S. copy editors.

So-called modern usage has come up with "spokesperson" for "spokesman" and "gay" for "homosexual." More than half the copy editors in the survey would still use "spokesman" and cross out "spokesperson." But only 13.5 percent would change "gay" to "homosexual," although many editors remarked how sorry they are to lose the excellent original meaning of "gay." Gene Foreman, managing editor of the Philadelphia Inquirer, put it this way: "I do not regard the above (the list of incorrect words), except for 'gay,' as 'modern usages.' They are incorrect usages!" The Cincinnati Enquirer editor added: "I'd call them modern misusages!"

Although there is no such real word as "disenfranchised (the correct word is "disfranchised"), half of the editors surveyed would let the former go because of its current wide usage.

Among other things that bother editors is a reporter who does not know the difference between "lie" and "lay" (from Hal Schellkopf of the Columbus (Ohio) Dispatch); "upcoming" and "downplay" (from William Kregar of the Wall Street Journal); "enthuse" as a verb (from Robert Ingle of the Miami-Herald); "Ms" for Miss or Mrs. (from Hobart Bucher of the (Peoria, Ill.) Journal Star and dozens of other editors); "looks like" (from scores of magazine and newspaper editors); "disinterested" for "uninterested" (from Dorothy Illson, copy chief of Fortune, and many others). A thoroughly disgusted editor from House & Garden put it quite simply for a great many editors: "There are too many to list!"

There was little difference between the response of newspaper and magazine copy chiefs, although several pointed out, that sports pages and publications concerned with racy subjects will often allow usage totally out of place on an editorial page or in the New Yorker.

Educational background also meant little this time, with 45.9 percent of those queried having been journalism majors in college and 52.7 percent non-majors (some did not respond).

Questionnaires were sent to editors of 50 randomly selected newspapers with circulations of 50,000 to 100,000; to 100 newspapers with circulations greater than 100,000; and to 40 leading magazines with circulations of 25,000 to more than 5,000,000.

USAGE SURVEY NO. 3: 'MS.' LOSING HEARTS AND/OR MINDS OF COPY EDITORS

Richard L. Tobin

"Ms." is rapidly losing its hold on the copydesks of America's top newspapers and magazines, according to the third annual English usage survey conducted by the School of Journalism at Indiana University.

The term had its heyday in the 1970s and for a time achieved great popularity here and in Great Britain. But only 57.3 percent of the copy chiefs responding to the latest IU usage survey would now leave it in, while 42.7 percent would edit it out. (Incidentally, more than half of those respondents who attended journalism schools would change "Ms.," while only thirty-five percent who did not have journalism training in college would do so, a statistic for which there is no immediate explanation.)

Susan B. Hahn, copy chief at *Time,* says: "We refer to a woman by her surname alone after the first identification by her full name. *Time* has never preceded the names of women or men with any form of address—Mr., Mrs., Miss, or Ms." Chris West, copy chief of the *Seattle Post-Intelligencer,* states that his paper doesn't use any of these forms except to avoid ambiguity. Dan Griffith of the *Washington Post* puts it this way: "In obituaries, *Post* style is to use 'Mr.' or 'Mrs.' or 'Miss,' but not, even if we have reason to believe that that's the individual's preference, 'Ms.' " Ann K. Wendt, chief of research at the *National Geographic,* says, however, that "it depends on the preference of the individual." And *The Times* of London now bans "Ms." entirely on the grounds that "it has no precise meaning."

Federalese is once again high on the hate list of the average copyreader. "The Federal budget cut will *impact* on a great many social services for minorities" would be changed by ninety percent of the copy desks responding to It's survey, while the use of nouns as verbs ("Union Carbide is now *officed* in Danbury") would be cut by 88.2 percent. Irving Kolodin, music critic of the *Saturday Review* and of *Newsday* says succinctly of "officed" or "headquartered" as verbs: "No!"

Allan M. Siegal, news editor of *The New York Times,* would change every one of the ten sentences quoted in this year's usage survey, examples taken from newspapers and magazines published during the past year. Only two of 120 respondents would let "He then told the frightened cashier to wait five minutes *inside of* the vault" stand without removing the "of." That 98.3-percent vote for change was the highest in this year's survey. Others that received more than ninety percent negative votes were "fortuitous" for "fortunate," "disinterested" for "uninterested," and "couple" instead of "couple of."

Use of "and/or" was disliked in its context by 64.2 percent, though several pointed out that there are times when "and/or" can be useful. The common expression in reporting military moves, "to within," rather than simply "within," didn't bother 66.7 percent of the respondents, though 33.3 percent would change it to "within" and four editors didn't care either way. The word "enormity" used to express size would be changed by 82.6 percent of the respondents on the ground that its basic meaning involves wickedness.

Several editors added their own pet peeves. The Peoria, Illinois, *Journal-Star* editor can't stand "compliment" for "complement," "monies" for "moneys," "marshall" for "marshal," and "over" for "more than," with the common misspelling of "supersede" ("supercede") most irritating of all. Hal Goodman, editor of *Psychology Today,* doesn't like the common use of "presently" for "currently," while several editors are still groaning about "like" used as a conjunction, an item in IU's first usage survey three years ago.

Thomas S. Barber, assistant news editor of *The Milwaukee Journal,* has this to say about modern usage: "I think 'changing fashion' is a charitable explanation for the examples you have asked editors to comment on in your 1981 English usage survey. I must admit that several of the blunders you've discovered would slip past many of our editors because of ignorance, not any new liberalism toward usage."

The 1981 survey

In 1979 and 1980 the journalism school of Indiana University surveyed more than two hundred major newspapers and magazines across America on the subject of changing fashions in language—words and phrases creeping into usage that have not up to now been accepted diction. Two years ago editors' pet hates were "like" as a conjunction, "less" instead of "fewer," and the split infinitive. Last year they were "different than" instead of "different from," "irregardless" for "irrespective" or "regardless," and any modification of "unique."

Again last fall many editors added their own pet peeves to the ones listed in the survey—so many, in fact, that the third national usage survey was based largely on suggestions from the nearly sixty percent who responded to the 1980 survey. These are included in the following list, all taken from newspapers and magazines published this past year. The survey drew 121 responses. Not all respondents answered every question.

1. *Enormity* used to express size. "The enormity of the crowd created a massive traffic jam near the stadium." (From Detroit paper).
   Let it go   17.4% (21)
   Change it   82.6% (100)
2. *Inside of* rather than *inside*. "He then told the frightened cashier to wait five minutes inside of the vault." (From Miami paper).
   Let it go   1.7% (2)
   Change it   98.3% (118)
3. *Couple* used instead of a *couple of*. "The Dodgers then came up with a couple doubles to tie the score." (From Los Angeles paper).
   Let it go   4.2% (5)
   Change it   95.8% (115)
4. *Ms.* instead of *Miss* or *Mrs.* "Ms. Turner was elected chairman by an overwhelming vote of the intersorority council." (From Columbus, Ohio paper).
   Let it go   57.3% (59)
   Change it   42.7% (44)
5. *Disinterested* instead of *uninterested*. "The judge was obviously disinterested in the defense attorney's argument." (From Missouri paper).
   Let it go   9.3% (11)
   Change it   90.7% (107)
6. *Fortuitous* for *fortunate*. "It was fortuitous that the driver was wide awake." (From Washington paper).
   Let it go   10.0% (12)
   Change it   90.0% (108)
7. *Nouns* used as *verbs*. "Union Carbide is now officed in Danbury, Conn."; "Time Inc. is headquartered in New York." (Both from New York financial publication).
   Let it go   11.8% (13)
   Change it   88.2% (97)
8. *And/or.* "The new rules would reduce the incidence of absenteeism and/or stealing." (From Oregon paper).
   Let it go   35.8% (43)
   Change it   64.2% (77)
9. *Impact* as a verb. "The Federal budget cut will impact on a great many social services for minorities." (From Washington speech text).
   Let it go   10.0% (12)
   Change it   90.0% (108)
10. *To within.* "Soviet troops have pushed tonight to within four miles of Kabul." (From wire service report).
    Let it go   66.7% (78)
    Change it   33.3% (39)
11. If you attended college, did you major in journalism at *either* the undergraduate or graduate level?
    Yes   47.8% (54)
    No   52.2% (59)